2/8/'09

Magician From The Masses

For Gordie,

Wishing you clarity
& ease.

In New Light

Alex

Alexandria E. Walsh-Roberts

Magician From The Masses

Mastering The Alchemy of Change

Alexandria E. Walsh-Roberts

LIFEOFLIGHT
MEDIA

Published by
LifeOfLight Media

www.lifeoflightmedia.com
info@lifeoflightmedia.com

ISBN: 0-908807-12-0

3

For my beloved, for Mother Earth
that is known as India and New Zealand,
and to all the Magicians from the Masses
who have helped me on the unfolding
path of alchemy —
10♦, 2♦, 9♣, K♦, 4♠, 3♦, 6♥,
10♣, 9♦, 3♣, A♥, 7♣, 6♦, K♣, J♥,
5♦, 3♠, Q♣, 4♣.

TABLE OF CONTENTS

The end of the beginning

"Is that you?" came a voice from the basement.

"Well that depends on which you you are looking for," I replied cheekily.

"You, of course," came the curt response as the discarnate voice made its way up the stairs and the puffing Mrs Daley shuffled into view.

"And there you are," I smiled… double locking my flat door. "And how would we be today?" I asked, reflecting her Irish curiosity. She stiffened with disapproval as if my kiss of the Blarney was less than authentic.

"Off again?" she questioned with a mixture of disapproval and rejection, as if in some way she would become a victim of my immanent departure.

"Well, if the truth were known, I've been off for years," I joked. "There's no use in trying to hide this any more. I'm going to come clean…" I lowered my voice… "just between you and me, you understand."

Mrs Daley lent forward as if guaranteeing her secrecy.

"I'm a travel junkie; an addict with no sign of recovery."

"Is that all? I thought it was something important!" she exclaimed.

"But I'm serious Mrs Daley. I can't stay in one place too long for fear of stagnation! My life is just one big mainline; whether it's a track, a road or a flight I've always got to be on it. Some may call it the way of the fool but it could actually be the way of the pilgrim," I suggested. Mrs Daley remained expressionless. "Some might even go as far as saying it's the journey that reveals the light at the end of the tunnel." I smiled. She didn't.

"Well whatever some may say, I think you're off your rocker. Young people these days just don't know when they're well off," she frowned.

"Perhaps that's true but I'm late, so I'll fly." I motioned

towards the door but stopped as Mrs Daley began another of her 'thoughts for the day.'

"Well, you've made your bed so you'll have to lie in it," she announced, scowling at my whimsical optimism.

"That may be true. But I'd prefer to think of my direction as simply an alternative avenue in the city of Life. Besides, I've got far too much living to do to be lying in a bed I haven't made! Perhaps it's not entirely unexpected, Mrs Daley. I am, after all, a travel journalist." I concluded my defense by wheeling my suitcase towards the front door.

But Mrs Daley wasn't finished yet. Launching into a determined waddle, she reached the mailboxes, blocking my escape. "Well, you can't be comfortable in a different hotel every night and with all those strange people," she persisted with her argument. "Don't you like the familiar?"

"Well Mrs Daley, you know what they say: familiarity breeds contempt."

My adversary fell silent. For the past five years she'd made it her personal mission to warn me of any risk, or near risk, I might be taking. But now her pursed lips confirmed that I was yet again beyond the point of no return. Fortunately for me, this meant our agreement would continue into its sixth year. I would buy Mrs Daley a gift from my foreign destination and in exchange she would stop interrogating me and start interrogating my flat while I was away. Who knew what 'ifs' could be lurking; unexpected visitors such as pigeons through my bathroom window; or the opportunity to make one of my many unclaimed lottery tickets crack under the pressure of its sixty-four million dollar secret.

Our familiar pause ended with Mrs Daley's attempted U-turn into sentimentality. "Well, don't be away too long. I can't look after your place forever." She stepped back as if signaling my departure.

"No, I quite understand. You've got better things to do with your life."

"Yes, and you'll do well to remember that. So don't let me hold you up… And don't go drinking the water and eating that foreign food." She paused as if she'd forgotten to tell me something. Instead she surprised me with a question. "Where are you going anyway?"

"India," I replied.

She paused, a broad smile parting her lips, excited at this last minute information and preparing herself for a late challenge.

"Oh, if its India you want, why do you have to go all that way on a plane when you can save your time and money and go round to VJ Singh's on the corner?" She glowed, believing she'd found a chink in my traveling amour.

"Well, you have to be there, Mrs Daley. That's what travel writing is all about. It's the spice of life; the thrill of the discovery. I'm after the original, the concentrated version, not something that has evolved into an intriguing hybrid. No offence intended, VJ."

Mrs Daley's logic, now punctured, was deflating fast. "Well, like I said, don't go drinking the water. God only knows what's in it."

"You're definitely right about that, Mrs Daley," I said, giving her the victory and recognition she wanted. "I'll see you when I get back. Thanks for looking after the place. Any ideas what you'd like me to bring back?"

"How about something I haven't got!" she replied, giving me a toothy grin.

"Okay. I'll get you something you can get your teeth into! Well, when you're wearing them, that is."

She went to slap my arm but instead turned her hand to receive the spare key to my three hundred square foot palace. "Don't go missing me now," I teased.

"I won't," she replied.

Opening the door, I flagged a cab, rushing down the front steps in a cloud of tardiness.

"Heathrow, please; Terminal Two. And can you step on it!"

"Certainly. Going anywhere nice?" asked the cab driver edging skillfully back into the traffic.

"On a trip of many lifetimes."

"Right you are," he said, giving me a strange look in the rear vision mirror.

Common ground

Nothing could have prepared me for my arrival at Mumbai Airport. My mind bombarded and exhausted itself with 'whys' by the time I'd arrived at the pre-paid taxi stand. My heart, meanwhile, was overwhelmed by the creative force of one billion members of the oldest order known to man—chaos.

It was easy to see why India got your attention and how your defenses and abilities combined to produce an unfamiliar, even alarming intensity. India was in a world of its own. You couldn't go over it, or around it. The only way was through this sensory overload, cramming itself within the bulging borders of the world's largest democracy.

My first twenty-six hours were spent in Second Class Aircon on the Udyan Express. The phrase 'Don't ask why' floated through a merge of sleeping and waking moments. The next morning at 11:35 I alighted in South India, forty-five minutes later than scheduled. Indian Standard Time had expanded to meet Indian Stretchy Time—and I was grateful for the change of pace.

Thursday came and went in a drowsy blur filled with suitcases and falling asleep at the slightest opportunity. My surroundings had caught up on me. As much as I tried to launch into my next assignment, India called me back to catch up with myself. No sooner had I started organizing my work than the day warped into late afternoon leaving me tired from doing nothing. By the fourth day I'd given up trying to organize or establish my direction, I simply surrendered.

The next sound I heard was my 8:30am alarm followed closely by the door bell. Who could that be? No one knows me here. But I was wrong; you were never alone in India. I opened the door to be greeted by the broadest of welcoming smiles.

"Good Morning. I am Prakash, the building manager. How are you settling in? Do you have everything you need? I promised the agency I would take particular care in ensuring you are comfortable."

"That's really kind, Prakash. To be honest, the place is a bit messy at the moment; don't know if I'm coming or going. Give me a few days and I'll tell you if there is anything I need help with. You'll be in the building?"

"Yes, yes. I am usually somewhere to be found. There is always some work to be done. Have you been out into town yet? Done a little shopping perhaps? India is full of bargains you know, beautiful bargains." I could guess what was coming next...

"As a matter of fact, my cousin-brother has a Kashmir emporium. It's very near to here. I could take you if you like."

"Oh that's really kind... but..." I began.

"It's no bother," Prakash continued in full flow. "A bit of research for your travel book. Maybe you could mention his emporium in your shopping section. He has the finest selection in Bangalore."

"Well thanks for the invitation. I wasn't actually planning on buying much here in India as I'm here to write. But you know that already."

"Yes of course. You are the travel writer from London," he smiled knowingly.

"Yes indeed. Well, back to my unpacking then," I hinted.

"Oh of course. I won't take up any more of your valuable time," he smiled walking to the lift. "Don't forget, if you'd like any help, I'm downstairs." He continued to smile his longest smile while descending in the lift.

"Well, well; the eternal bargain," I mused, closing the door and walking into the kitchen. "Perhaps it's time I traversed the ancient trade routes and discovered the heart of Indian shopping."

I stopped stock still in the kitchen. Something was different... I wasn't tired any more. So maybe it was time for some retail therapy? I could even kill two birds with one stone — buying Mrs Daley's gift while starting my research. It was a tempting efficiency. I would find an oriental gem; one to match the gem of the Emerald Isle who was now in my flat watching satellite TV while slowly emptying the fridge of stout.

Retail therapy

I never thought I'd find God in a jewelry shop. But the narrow frontage before me, decorated in bright colors and traditional symbols, hinted otherwise. I was now off the tourist beaten track in an area of town called Commercial Street. The street was narrow but it's appeal was broad. This was true shopping where the variety was less predictable, as was the price. The characters that created legend, deception and illumination all worked here, trading dreams and tragedies at an everyday price. It was becoming increasingly obvious that this wasn't the King's Road or Fifth Avenue, it was India. Logic didn't work here in a collage of chaos glued together with faith. But God's color, ceremony, mystery and chaos carried on without a hitch.

Sandwiched between its up-and-coming jeans-selling cousins, this tiny jewelry shop was packed full of an air of conscious consumerism as shoppers discussed the advice of their marriage astrologer or simply how they were going to guarantee good fortune with the help of Topaz, Peridot and Ruby.

Moving deeper into the shop, I squeezed past a human Tower of Pisa precariously wavering from side to side while trying on toe rings. Balancing on a stool in front of a cabinet of assorted jewelry, I began scanning for a pendant. Crystals and semiprecious stones had been one of my passions for many years but today nothing caught my eye. I tried to picture Mrs Daley with a delicate design in Garnet but the picture wouldn't come into focus. I looked again into my present's future. Perhaps Mrs Daley would surprise and delight me in ethnic silver fringes of the Indian Hill Tribes. The picture burst suddenly like a thought bubble from a cartoon. "Maybe not," I muttered.

As I continued to peer anxiously into the display case, the shop owner zeroed in on my frustration. Sensing my rapidly scattering purchasing power, he caught my eye.

"Can I show you anything?" he gestured towards the display case.

"Well, I'm looking for a pendant," I replied. "I wanted a Garnet for my friend. It's really weird as I can normally find what I want but not today… There's such a wide selection and yet still nothing similar to what I had in mind."

"What about these?" My co-seeker ushered out his best assortment. "Do you only want Garnet or can I show you other stones?" The jeweler's search was about to broaden.

"No thanks," I sighed. "I've set my heart on Garnet."

"Well," the shop owner sat back on his stool, "there's no point in arguing with the heart."

"Perhaps I should ask for some divine intervention?" I said half joking, half hoping.

"Well, if you were going to ask anyone, God would be the one because that's the Universal Wholesaler who supplies everything."

"What do you mean?"

The shopkeeper took a deep breath filled with pride. He wobbled slightly on his stool. His laughing Buddha physique was perched in the middle of commercial mayhem, he glowed as he began to enlighten me with his theories on Life, the Universe and shopping.

"The Force, whether you call it Rama, God, 'Out There' or 'All-That-Is' can be seen as a Universal Wholesaler who has all the products ever imagined in our world plus many we have yet to dream of. There is no limit to what we can buy nor to our purchasing power. But this Wholesaler won't force us to buy; all purchases come from free will and free will alone."

He paused for effect and it worked. I nodded my agreement, now a willing student of free will. He cleared his throat and continued.

"The Universal Wholesaler sells familiar commodities of this physical world such as jewelry, houses, kitchenware, good health, books and cars. You name it and it's there. Even the more elusive aspects of our world are available such as peace, unconditional love, joy and wisdom. It doesn't matter whether we understand the full extent of what is on offer, it's still available whether we want it or not."

He paused to pass a tray of anklets to his colleague, and continued.

"What we want to buy is entirely up to us as the Universal Wholesaler has an unlimited supply and has no interest in convincing us to buy anything in particular."

That sentence hit home with the old 'one-two'; first a punch of simplicity, then one of honesty. It sent my brain reeling. I couldn't remember the last time I'd been shopping and not felt pressured to buy something. Advertising, ambient music and buy-one-get-one-free had been shouting increasingly louder with each passing year. Did I buy because I wanted to or because the environment told me to?

The jeweler continued, engrossed in his theory.

"All we are required to do is choose what we want. All

requests are dealt with equally. Moreover, the Universal Wholesaler will supply everything at an affordable price irrespective of the quantity."

Pausing for a moment, he leant forward as if building up to a dramatic conclusion.

"There is only one trading condition — anyone buying from the Universal Wholesaler cannot return the goods nor blame anyone for bad service, bad quality or the form their request takes in their world. All customers are 100% responsible for what they've chosen. It's their soul responsibility to discover how this new range of products is going to fit into their world and if it can co-exist alongside all the items that already make up their brand of life. Sourcing direct from the Universal Wholesaler is the Heart of *real life*. It's the genuine article, whereas Retail is just something that we've got used to because it appears easier."

"Sorry, you're losing me. What do you mean exactly?"

The jeweler slowed his enthusiasm to increase clarity.

"Retail comes in a box wrapped up in definition. But you can't put life in a box — it doesn't have defined limits. There are so many variations that no single box will ever fit. So Retail belongs to a limited version of Life, a comfortable compromise where one size fits all. It's easy, relatively inexpensive and perfectly adequate; it supplies what you think you want. Whereas the Universal Wholesaler helps you create what you *really* want in your heart and in your life. The cost is greater in the short term but the benefits far exceed your initial investment."

My jewelry guru relaxed as if he'd made his point. Smiling with a hint of smugness, he leaned back against the shelf behind, satisfied with the sale he'd made, even if it was only an idea.

"Maybe it's time to ask the Universal Wholesaler for what you really want," he smiled. "There's no reason to settle for less. No reason at all."

"Sounds like a fantastic idea," I agreed enthusiastically.

This got me thinking. 'How about putting clarity at the

top of my shopping list?' I thought. 'These concepts are mind blowing, even life changing!'

The jeweler concluded his deluge of realization…

"It's more than an idea, you know, it's a way of life." He paused. "But perhaps I'm lucky that most people don't take it seriously! It's hard enough to hear your thoughts in this world let alone find out what's behind them."

The owner chuckled, his large paunch emphasizing his humorous gems of wisdom. I didn't hear the joke but got carried away by infectious laughter, until tears welled in my eyes.

"Well," I said as the laughter subsided, "thanks for the inspiration. I haven't laughed like that in a long time. Off I go now to discover what's beyond Retail."

"Can you remember what you wanted?" He looked intently into my eyes.

"Now that you ask me, I haven't got a clue. You've blown my mind and now all I have is a huge void!"

"Well, don't worry," he smiled warmly. "Keep searching. You'll find your gift soon enough."

Just then as if the space were only staying open long enough for the shop owner to finish his sentence, he was swallowed up in a new wave of demands for earrings, American diamonds and friendship bracelets. Meanwhile, I was washed back out through the door, cleansed of my failed consumerism and now energizing my thoughts in a completely new spin cycle.

The gift of uncertainty

I stood in the street, caught in a cloud of dust and bewilderment. Everything around me appeared to be accelerating like a video on fast-forward. I had been left behind. My train of thought had stopped in a station I didn't recognize; there was noise and muffled announcements but nothing made sense. I felt strangely disconnected, suddenly an outsider enveloped in a bubble of slow motion, struggling to remain in contact with my surroundings.

Sitting down with a dull thud on the pavement a wave of energy traveled through my body draining through my feet into the ground. Everything was too much, too quick. I stopped thinking, stopped moving, just sat. A succession of distorted images passed my view until my focus returned and I became the sitting target of a boy selling wooden cobras.

A harassed grimace was enough to chase away the souvenir seller and my disorientation began to dissolve. The street slowed to normal, whatever that was, and I began to speed up to meet it. At last I was feeling more like myself.

I decided to go home via the open air market. But, as I got up to leave, my feet mutinied, walking me straight across the road to a European-style coffee shop. I had neither the presence of mind nor the will to protest. If there was one aspect of life India had taught me already, it was to go with the flow. There was always more time in time than there first appeared.

The back corner of the café beckoned me over to settle with my large cappuccino. I stared into the heart shape that had been carefully etched into my cappuccino foam. I scooped it up in my spoon and drank it. As soon as its essence entered my nervous system I felt revived. Questions and inspiration began jostling for position as my mind got back into gear. I waited until I could hear myself think and began reviewing my obviously changing world.

Using the jeweler's analogy, I had been sourcing the majority of my reality from 'Retail.' I wrote 'Retail' on a serviette in capital letters.

I'd been unaware of the potential of my heart because it wasn't part of the world of Retail. I'd been occupied with what was in front of me rather than what was within me.

This had been working well up until now; there had always been something in my immediate vicinity that was a close match to what I thought I wanted so I'd settled for that. I'd become dependent on the middlemen: societies, religions, monarchies and bureaucracies to define my world for me. Being told what I could and couldn't do had become a form of comfort, something that made my world more certain even dependable. I decided to call this world Existence. I drew a large cube with the word 'Existence' in the center of it.

In Existence I could unburden myself of the responsibility of choice by allowing the structures around me to make my choices for me. If I didn't like what I received I could simply blame the middlemen for not coming up with the goods. Alternatively, I could go and buy a replacement to stem any upsurge of dissatisfaction. Existence became a dependable provider because there was increasingly less choices as variety diminished. If your level of satisfaction was relatively constant, there didn't appear to be much point in seeking an alternative. Why start working out what you could or couldn't do when Existence was more than qualified to do it for you?

The more I thought about the limits of Existence, the easier it was to see how you could get sucked into a choice-vacuum as Existence's hold became more and more secure. There was no way out because there were no alternatives. Everything was spiraling into control with no room for change. Existence would then stagnate into a controlled certitude that demanded more and more control to keep the same level of satisfaction. The ultimate Existence was letting your environment decide everything for you while you relinquished any creative choice or responsibility.

Perhaps if I'd thought about this before I would have laughed off a complete loss of creativity and responsibility as impossible.

"Don't be stupid; who was going to buy into that?"

I'd hear myself say. "That could never happen, really. It's just a model, a study of human behavior taken to some theoretical extreme."

But today I was beginning to see how I could be tempted to fit into that model. It did, after all, offer comfort, security and dependability. Changing all that for the sake of choice suddenly seemed less important.

I stopped scribbling and looked around the café walls. Was I in Existence right now? Was this a box within a box? I felt uncomfortable, hemmed in by the thought that I was existing in a compromise which gave me less choice with each effort. My discomfort intensified when I looked back at my last five years and how I'd started to write to the formula which brought me the most stability instead of the most joy. There was a part of me that had fallen into Existence, it was just that I'd been too busy to notice. Now I understood what had happened. India hadn't just brought me to a coffee shop, it had helped me move beyond my comfort zone. I'd got through my disorientation so I could find a change of direction. Now I was actually listening to myself, even if at first I didn't like what I heard.

It was time for a change and I wasn't going to find it in Existence. My coffee and realizations had sobered me up so I could see just how much of my world was created from control and lack and how much from love and trust. If I wanted to fall in love with writing again it was time to explore outside the cube; give up the formula of Existence and enter a world filled with expansion, purpose and uncertainty.

The traffic noise suddenly intensified, drawing my attention through the shop front into the busy street. Life was right before my eyes in all its bustling glory; indefinable and endless. No one fear or limit could capture the world through my window. I smiled at how perfect my view was. This unending flow of uncertainty was just the kind of disturbance I needed to jolt me out of my control lethargy. Now I'd found my feet, I welcomed alternatives. I wanted to stop clinging to what I knew and start rediscovering spontaneity. I hadn't just crossed over the road, I'd left Existence in search of Life.

I drew a large circle on a new serviette and wrote 'LIFE' inside in capital letters. So what made Life different to Existence? The short answer—choice and uncertainty. Life had as many alternatives as you were prepared to accept; the flow was unending. Just when you'd thought of everything, Life showed you an extra piece of everything. Guidelines replaced limits in a flexi-structure that responded to your every discovery.

Life didn't want to shelter you from learning nor prevent you from discovering the reason for your choices. Life encouraged you to sense your world, feel your level of fulfillment and explore what could be, rather than what had been tried and tested. In Life, the unknown wasn't rejected because it was unfamiliar, it was explored for its potential.

Taking a third serviette I drew, Existence and Control on the left hand side in a cube and Life and Choice in a circle on the right hand side. If I started out in Existence then, when I chose differently, I would leave the cube and progress into the circle of Life. If I was in Life and began to reject choice, fearing rather than trusting, I would move back towards the limits and controls of Existence. This dynamic equilibrium was always changing to reflect how much I was Existing and how much I was living. The more I took responsibility for my choices, the more Life I would create; the more fear and control I endorsed, the more Existence I would reinforce.

Where was I in the equation? How much of me was Existing and how much Living? Perhaps it was 60:40, or 85:15. How could I know exactly? I stopped my analysis. There was the Existing part of me again, trying to evaluate limits instead of releasing me from them.

I felt someone trying to catch my attention. The coffee shop was closing. I paid and when I stood up to leave, my gift appeared on the table in front of me, just as the jeweler had promised. I hadn't expected a pile of serviettes but that didn't matter. I now had a scribbled train of thought that gave me a ticket to ride; destination, Life. And, more importantly, a mode of transport—choice.

Tired and tested

The afternoon monsoon was about to start. The air was taught, holding back the growing weight of humidity. Bulging droplets of rain burst on the pavement and began chasing me home. As I hurried through the open-air market, the traders were scrambling to protect their products with plastic sheets and bulldog clips. I turned my collar up and quickened my pace, glancing at the disappearing cones of colored powder, pyramids of vegetables and alleyways draped with sarees. Narrowly avoiding a brush with a very reasonably-priced Kashmiri shawl, I ducked into the apartment entrance as the monsoon pressure broke, releasing cascades of warm rain. I could still hear the overflow pipes delivering their deluge as I closed my front door.

Suddenly a wave of tiredness hit me. "I'll just lie down for a few minutes," I slurred drowsily.

Two and a half hours later I awoke to a fading dusk. The Imam was calling the faithful to prayer and the evening rush hour was gaining momentum. By the time I felt fully awake I found myself surrounded by darkness. The view out onto the street was one of pitch black, sparsely punctuated by handheld gas- and solar-powered lanterns. I turned the light on but nothing happened.

"Must be a power cut," I muttered to myself. I fumbled around for the candle beside the bed and coaxed a small flame which gradually began to light the room.

My eyes had now acclimatized to the few lights that

were available. I gravitated to the balcony and looked at the shadows cast by the small lamps in the houses opposite. Headlights threw beams that lit up surprised pedestrians as they clambered over the hidden obstacles on half-finished pavements.

There was a festive atmosphere in the Shanti Sagar Hotel at the end of the street. A step-down transformer on the opposite side of the road appeared to be the center of the power cut. Angrily, it spat blue and white sparks in the direction of onlookers from behind its rusty iron cage. A sudden influx of snackers were taking advantage of the establishment's ring side view and its oil powered generator that lit the dining area with a loud groan.

While standing on the balcony, I had become dinner for what appeared to be hordes of mosquitoes. In reality there were only two or three but they were enough to chase me back into the bedroom. How could something so small produce something so irritating? I was getting into full moan mode, vigorously scratching the bites on my feet and ankles with no apparent relief. 'Power cuts. Who needs them?' I thought. 'They're like unwanted visitors limiting what you can do and you never knew how long they are going to stay.'

I sat back on my bed and thought about what could be created with one candlepower. Shakespeare had written some of his thirty-seven plays by candlelight; some of the greatest inventors and visionaries had only known candlelight. So why should I allow my environment to dictate my creativity? My ability hadn't changed, just my surroundings. It was time to stop automatically assuming that when things didn't go the way you expected, they were unhelpful.

If the flow of Life was always changing moment to moment then expectations were always coming and going. They were never truly part of the present because they were always linked to the rationale of the past. If I stayed with expectation, I would continue to think of this time as an unproductive nuisance. I would be powerless, stranded in the past waiting for something to happen when there were plenty of alternatives to be found in the present.

What an irony—with no light I could actually see more clearly. The darkened surroundings had given me the contrast I required to understand that everything was a matter of perception. The days of Existence, when my experience was a predictable dot-to-dot, were dissolving. I no longer wanted to lock my activities in to a chain of consequences. You've got no light so, as a consequence, you can't do anything; you've done this so now you've got to do that. I wanted to liberate myself by acknowledging the opportunities I had at each creative juncture; 360 degrees of choice to be precise.

Creation carried on whether I perceived myself to be capable of it or not. I didn't necessarily create more because I did more. The way I would become more creative was through embracing the opportunities that came my way. It could easily blame India for this interruption in my doing but it was no one's fault and nothing was wrong. I was the only one who could stand in the way of my own creativity. In India it was never a question of things not working out, it was simply that they didn't necessarily work the way you expected they would.

I closed my eyes and listened to the sounds coming from the street. Wisps of broken sentences and fuzzy images from the day's activities began to reform in my mind's eye. I'd laughed 'til I'd cried in the jewelry shop, questioned my way to the bottom of two cappuccinos and, last but by no means least, I'd begun discovering the difference between Existence and Life.

What many would regard as a lot of irrelevant 'nothings' was so much more meaningful than any of the 'somethings' I'd considered important before. But how it was all going to help my writing I had no idea. Still I was happy to be ignorant.

My fractured mentality would mend soon enough. Having no plan meant I was literarily free!

Besides, de-mystifying travel by herding my research into neat paragraphs wasn't enough. It hadn't been anywhere near enough for a couple of years. The fun had leaked through the carefully crafted budget practicalities and out the other side. I was at a cross roads, in the dark! For the first time in my travel writing career I didn't want to plan a water tight foreign holiday, I wanted to relate a journey. No more editing out the excess and the extras, I wanted to leave them where they were — all part of the adventure of travel.

Walking home that afternoon, I'd had the ideal opportunity to try out some of my new theories when I came face to face with an incredibly cheap Kashmir shawl. Forgetting all my travel guide advice, I'd embraced the situation instead of avoiding it. It wasn't so much a question of to buy or not to buy, it was more the reasoning behind my choice. Buying it because it was cheap or because I didn't want to disappoint the salesman would have been Existing. Instead I left the shop empty handed because I chose Life. The reason I didn't buy the shawl was because I didn't want it. It was simple. Basing my decision on the fear of losing out on something I didn't actually want was so ridiculous it was funny.

I congratulated myself on refusing to let something that I didn't want control me. But as soon as I'd thought it, the memories of the times when I'd done exactly that came flooding back. How often had I let my environment or conditioning decide, creating through the fear of losing approval, love or control? A lack of choice had definitely been alive and well in my past. It had been much more complicated but a lot easier. Perhaps conditioning could let you fall backwards into the security of what you knew. That way you were out of the potential danger of learning.

So today I'd left a part of my past and my existence

behind. But what was the one element that linked everything together? I had no idea. I reached for my Rubik's cube, tucked under the bed; my old faithful that I had never solved but that had always helped me. I arranged some of the blue rows while taking my mind off my question. Dilute one problem by concentrating on another. Three more blue squares and I had the beginning of an answer.

Today... I'd felt my way rather than thinking it through. Thinking inside the cube had given me boxes within boxes. My mind had a category for everything, defining, dividing and limiting; an abundance of can'ts, won'ts, shouldn'ts and oughts. The logical mind had an explanation for every aspect of my Existence, but that was its limit.

India, on the other hand, allowed logic to find its place in the chaos of constant change. All was possible, just not logical. Here I had shifted the center of my world. Moving from the West to the East, I'd left a land dominated by the logical mind to a place ruled by the Heart. I was getting a 'feeling work-out.' Whether it was drama, joy, guilt or love, India had it all. I'd been climbing out of logic so I could reach this thought plateau and admire the feeling that had got me here. I was at peace, happy to let my Heart do the leading from now on. I'd left logic behind because it couldn't contain or understand the information I'd discovered in Life. All it could do was analyze it to death.

The Kingdom of Logic was just another part of Existence unwilling to co-create with the unknown because it was so interested in controlling it. Existence and Life spoke entirely different languages and I was beginning to experience a breakdown in communication between the world I'd known and the one I was discovering. What I now wanted made complete sense to my Heart and nonsense to my logical mind. Now I understood why things were falling apart — so they could come together.

"Thanks cube. The answer to all these questions is the

Heart," I nodded in recognition. "All these changes were connected and interconnected through the Heart. No logic could ever embrace my incredible journey so far. So what do you think about that?" I challenged the cube precociously. But it maintained its multi-colored silence.

My candle-length discussion was complete and with a spitting finale the flame extinguished itself. There was silence and darkness. "Time to move on. I've been in the dark long enough," I acknowledged. And with that, the fridge shuddered into life and the lights came back on.

Joining the land of the living

As the power was restored, so was the chaos. The evening rains were over and the streets were quickly packed with carts, carriages, cars and cows. As I looked from the balcony I was fascinated by a cow standing fast asleep amongst the traffic, taking a break from it's evening pilgrimage to the vegetable bins. Surely that was a tonne of trust, standing stock still in the middle of a stream of uncertainty. But for cows, the road less traveled was normal. They didn't worry about being hurt or starving, they simply mooed with the flow, quietly aware that there was more to Life than making it pass more quickly.

Clarity was hungry work and I decided to take the cow's cue and join the flow of commuting snackers going in the direction of Shanti Sagar Hotel. Walking purposefully up the street I made progress with surprising ease, unifying my intention and action had produced really fast food. I arrived at the hotel and had just secured a seat when the waiter came from the kitchen, menu in hand.

"Masala dosa, please," I said quickly. He nodded, acknowledging my choice.

"Chai?"

"Yes please. Good idea. I'll have a chai too."

After a few minutes the waiter returned with a triangular parcel stuffed with spicy potato filling. I tore off strips of the pancake and drowned it in coconut sauce. This was snack heaven. In South India, my minimal cooking skills had become a positive asset providing the perfect excuse to indulge my snacking habit. This was, of course, all in the name of travel guide research.

As I sat in the middle of the 7 p.m. snack traffic, the restaurant filled with every possible patron: families of young and old; businessmen comparing their latest account sheets; students and work colleagues discussing exam results, marriage proposals and pay rises; all navigating through their own flow of uncertainty to converge in this place.

I felt as if I was in the middle of a social fractal—the more I looked into the crowds, the more people I saw. I never felt so much a part of a group of strangers in my life.

The part of me in Existence tried to grab my attention as if anxious to stop me soaking up the bustling unity. 'There's no such thing as Cosmic patterns or a glue of Humanity that binds you all together,' it niggled. 'Forget the deep and meaningful; this is just a group of meetings and agreements. All can be explained logically.' But my mind had lost me. No equation could faithfully describe what was going on around me. You could feel it but you couldn't calculate it. For all I knew, each individual had come here on the spur of the moment.

'Stop nagging me into thought submission,' I protested in my mind. 'I don't want to focus on one solution to an imaginary equation. I can't know it all and, more importantly, I don't care if I have your solutions or not. If I'd listened to your assessments, I wouldn't even have bothered to come out at this time and I would have missed all this. I believe anything is possible and I'm prepared to take the risk.'

I was having a great time rebelling against the realistic.

I was tired of normal and general. I wanted abnormal, exceptional and individual. Questioning my mentality stretched its logic to breaking point. It snapped and fell silent; no more nagging objections and no more single lane logic. Existence might hold some interesting questions but Life was where I was going to find multiple answers.

High on enthusiasm and caffeine, I paid the bill and thanked Life for providing such stimulating company. With a head full of atmosphere and characters I returned home, settling on the balcony to continue my observations with a bird's eye view.

Indian traffic became the next Life study. It defied logic and mathematical probability, but it worked. Thousands upon thousands of minor flexibilities contributed to the miracle that was just another peak rush hour. Obstacle and space alike became the flow. It was impossible to think how this human monster wave arrived at the shores of work and home each day—there was no single explanation. But it highlighted logic's greatest flaw—just because it couldn't be worked out didn't mean it wouldn't work out.

The flow and activity of the crowds were putting me in the mood for writing. But with one major difference—I had no destination for my incoming paragraph. It stopped at the tip of my tongue waiting for a vehicle of expression. I quickly broke open a ream of paper I'd left on the balcony chair and started to write, I didn't know what. For the first time since I could remember I wrote without a point. Instead I wrote with an intention; honoring what was flowing through my head.

'Getting out of a rut,' I began, 'means going with the flow.' I paused and moved to the next line.

'Listening to yourself doesn't mean you tell yourself what you want to hear.'

'Surpassing Existence means going through the fear that there isn't anything beyond it.'

'If Life is the next step, so liberating, enlivening and expansive, *why isn't it more popular?' Why aren't more people getting a Life instead of sticking to Existence?'*

My pen stopped. I was distracted by the familiar tone of a scratched 45, a drifting crackle of 60's sparkle making its way through the commuting crowds. Glancing down towards the Ayuvedic Clinic, I saw Vinod arranging his collection of would-be antiques and curiosities, whose histories and prices he would embellish to epic proportions. Prakash had introduced me to this legendary eccentric as another local treasure he assured me would find its way into my book. Vinod was there every weekday night demonstrating the splendor of 'by gone' or 'near by gone' including a lava lamp which he knew I was secretly toying with buying.

Lava lamps' brash colors and endless flow of unpredictable shapes always reminded me of my favorite near history—the 60's. Nearly everyone I'd ever met who'd lived through the 60's seemed to be passionate about the decade, even those who detested it. There was no doubt that it was a choice explosion that rocked global inertia and stability alike. Whether you needed Help or Love, the Beatles were there to provide the backing. Suddenly experimentation was trendy and open-mindedness an asset rather than something that, with time, everyone would devalue and dismiss through cynicism.

So could the 60's tell me why the Life chain-reaction fizzled out? Come to think of it, what had happened to all the free love and free thinking? Nothing. The momentum behind alternatives never came forward to fuel permanent change. The vital ingredient—commitment—was missing.

Flower Power bloomed, wilted and dried up because it remained a nice idea at the time rather than becoming a reality. Conditioning told us the freak wave of mass creativity would end its disruption and find its level, dissolving within Existence rather than Life. Who wanted to invest in an unpredictable dream when you could have a comfortable status quo? Dependables such as struggle, denial, safety, need and doubt were far too precious to relinquish. At least you knew where you were in Existence. It didn't ask you to commit and be responsible because it had control. How could you create tangible fulfillment through intangibles such as trust and love?

I glanced at my unfinished Rubik's cube—the unending experiment; a work in progress that perhaps I'd never finish. But maybe I'd never committed to undergoing the process. My Cube wasn't hiding anything, just waiting for me to convert the idea of finishing it into reality.

Perhaps it was the same with the 60's. It marked the start of something that hadn't been completed yet. The choice experience wasn't so much a short story, more of a novel unfolding as each passing decade contributed new chapters. You could call it 'From Limitation to Liberation - an evolution through responsible change.'

The 70's had twisted and turned in the after shocks of the 60's. Frustrated and escapist, it overflowed with questions but found few answers. When the 80's delivered only superficial fulfillment we spent the 90's searching for the genuine article. The new millennium relaunched the hope that we could learn from our world and finally write the closing chapter of our experience in Limitation.

But just like my brief Rubik's cube experience, it was all still a matter of choice and commitment; a choice to end history repeating itself and the commitment to replace a lack of fulfillment with what really made the heart sing.

Slowing down to speed up

The reality of my own commitment was now hitting home. If I wanted to fill my creative space differently, I too was required to choose from the alternatives before me. My mind had been flashing neon deadlines, worries and obligation signs for over three days. "Get on with the reason you came!" "Start your book." "What's your editor going to say?"

But I'd paid no attention to these faint signs of panic. I felt sure that my new approach to writing was more than a lethargic detour. My gut feeling was telling me it would give this next commission a new twist, something that could spice up the tried and tested and take my work to a whole new level.

There was a sudden desire to be without limits, have a free flow of inspiration and yet, ironically, I was still searching for the start line to guarantee I had begun, and a sign post to confirm to me the right direction. I felt awkward; this 'experienced traveler' hadn't been here before.

I cast a glance at the telephone on the lounge table. It could ring at any moment, particularly as I hadn't called my editor since I'd arrived. The kettle voiced my frustration as it came to the boil and began letting off steam. What was I going to do? Return to Existence or surrender to change? The kettle's song increased to a shrill tone. I was beginning to think myself into anxiety; another mental detour I could do without.

"Time to slow down this mental overdrive!" I said scathingly.

The pot of Earl Grey was ready. I placed it on the living room table and collapsed into the sofa. There was a sound of creasing paper and something sticking into my spine. I found a couple of sheets of paper under the cushion behind my head and sticking out of the sofa back was the pen I'd misplaced only a few days before.

My usual reaction would be to get control, gather my actions into some sort of plan… So I decided not to. Instead I'd commit to guidelines. Seeking refuge in my past approach was only compounding my resistance and confusion rather than giving me the breakthrough I was searching for. I wrote guidelines at the top of the page.

One: Unplug head, get off mental merry-go-round.

Two: Reroute all choices through the heart, no exceptions. I'd create for the love of it, not through trying to keep my world under control, in fear or lack.

My view of time appeared to be putting me under the most amount of pressure so I would choose to replace Indian Standard Time permanently with Indian Stretchy Time. The stress of deadlines was sapping my energy. I was attempting to re-create my approach to work without changing the structure.

It was time to consult the library of conditioning. I sifted through its shelves until I arrived at the box marked *Time*. I began to assess its entries. They were too numerous to count. 'I don't have time for this' I began. But I stopped, if I was going to work differently I had to make time to change. I read some of the entries: directives such as *You have to work hard for everything you have; Cram time until it can't hold anymore; Understand that, above all, there is a direct relationship between what you achieve and how long you spend doing it; The longer you work, the more you will get or the better your work will be.* It's that simple, conditioning told me. What are you waiting for?

It was becoming obvious that it was actually that *strugglesome*. Change was definitely worth slowing down for. No amount of time in itself would add value to my creativity. Every time I put myself under pressure to fill time, the reason had been that I feared losing it or wasting it. Sometimes I thought I could beat time by trying to keep some up my sleeve! Why? Because if I had more time it would automatically make me more creative... "What a waste of time that conditioning has been," I acknowledged as I scribbled.

I knew time was a limit, just like scarcity and targets, and keeping within it meant your creativity couldn't expand, only be curbed. So from now on I would step outside of it. If there was no time, there was no struggle fitting into it and there was no more fearing the lack of it. These were all limits I could do and be without. I didn't have to work hard for everything that I produced, all I was required to do was commit to the creativity rather than the limits that I'd imposed around it. I would be well occupied rather than preoccupied with what I might be unable to do.

Guideline Three read: *Don't do time, embrace now.* Less limits, as far as I could see, meant more flow. If I could recognize the flow then I'd have many more alternatives. My discussion with the jeweler had been an incoming flow; my connection with India was another; Prakash's sales pitch another. My Heart told me there were as many ways and directions as I was prepared to allow. In fact there were more ways than I could ever fathom. All I was required to be was open.

Just because I didn't know an opportunity of a lifetime was flowing right towards me at that moment didn't mean I couldn't be open to it when it arrived. My new book was arriving as I wrote. Its direction and route were unknown but that didn't stop its arrival. Only my lack of openness would limit the flow — clinging to the past and to what I thought was possible instead of embracing what was actually possible at that moment.

I sat up and poured some tea. This was a genuine flow. I had everything I required in that moment. Tea, paper, pen and ideas. It was an uplifting sensation full of productivity and fulfillment. And yet it hadn't taken the hours it might have suggested. I felt like I was beginning to understand what it was really like to be abundant — to create everything you wanted in each moment. I brought my attention back to the page in front of me and guideline number four.

Four: Trade in the need to know for the ability to trust. Ignorance is bliss! Stop fighting to know and allow the flow to show. Everything was in front of me, not behind me and certainly not beyond me. I didn't need to dash into what-ifs and maybes to ambush my progress with a fearful future. Each moment was a perfect source of inspiration and answers. Like a perfect bubble, it held no consequences or sequences. The moment wasn't asking me to slide up and down a fixed track, back and forth between 'then' and 'will be'. 'Now' gave me all the directions and all the choices I ever needed to know.

Five: Quality time with self is valuable flow time. It was helping clear conditioning and limits as they became obvious. It was the balancing factor in allowing, understanding and co-creating. The flow would never appear too much or too little if you made time to flow with yourself and made space to collect your own answers. I couldn't ask the Universe to fix my problems but by being with myself I could nurture the understanding to solve them with its help.

Six: Discover alternative sources of inspiration by keeping the door to the Heart open at all times, even if it is seriously tempting to slam it shut.

These wisdom workouts created more tools to produce Life and more ways to keep retrieving the parts of self still in Existence.

My internal revolution was taking shape. The tea and the meeting were completed. I took a cloth to wipe up the drips from the teapot as they rapidly merged with the serviettes from the coffee shop. The tea drops were beginning to blur the inky limits of the Existence of two days before. How different the serviettes appeared now as barriers dissolved and the guidelines of Life began to dismantle the limiting boundaries of Existence.

I sat back on the sofa beginning to re-read the pages I'd just written. The phrase 'discovering alternative sources of inspiration' jumped out at me. I couldn't think of anything. So I stopped thinking and asked my Heart. A message floated upward, landing with a gentle thud in the center of my third eye. It read 'Meditation'.

"Well, signs don't come any more obvious than that," I

replied out loud. "I'll give it a go." As the sound of commitment faded, so did the sign. I was empty—no mind babble, no thoughts, just space and the invitation of flow.

It was hard to believe but 'Doing nothing' was my first leap into the unknown. Still, I'd done a few local yoga classes and attended some relaxation groups. I could repeat what I'd done there and see what happened.

Closing my eyes, I felt strangely self conscious and I wanted to laugh. So I did. I laughed as if bubbles of fizzy drink were lodged in my nose. My concentration collapsed and I opened my eyes. The room was still there; it was now about five minutes later than when I'd started.

My lack of concentration must be because of the way I was sitting. I went and sat on the floor with my back against the wall to support my flagging self discipline and posture. I closed my eyes once more. All I could hear was the sound of traffic horns on their way to work and shop owners lifting their iron grills preparing to open for business. But instead of reacting and blaming the sounds for my lack of concentration, my mind had no comments, just silence.

I stopped fighting the flow of sound and let go, moving further and further into the space within the cacophony. I began to waver between feeling heavy and light. There was warmth in the right side of my body, concentrated around my right shoulder. I was adrift… my feet were tingling and I could no longer sense my physical body. Someone had turned down the traffic noise and I could hear the sound of people speaking English. The discussion was a noisy mutter, too quiet to be understood and yet loud enough to be intriguing. I decided to interject.

"Are you talking to me?" I asked.

"Well, I thought you had some questions," came the reply. "Wasn't that the idea of this get-together—you wanted to get started in Life? ...Shake up a cocktail of limited and unlimited experiences? ...Resuscitate your taste buds so you

Magician From The Masses

can begin tasting the difference? So what will it be? —a shot of the concentrated stuff?"

"Well, isn't it a bit early for that? I don't know if I'm completely acclimatized yet. Perhaps something with a little less kick. I'll admit Existence has become tasteless and I do want a change, spice things up a little. But I think it's better that I start with something light. What about a mocktail, please? Something that's got a bit of Life and a bit of Existence. I'm not ready for the neat stuff just quite yet."

"Okay. One Mocktail coming up," came the reply as a presence oscillated in front of me, just out of focus. I certainly wasn't drunk but being in this place made me light-headed. There were no precise forms but everything had an intriguing feel to it. It was like being in a bar but they were serving concepts rather than drinks.

"So what's your story?" I asked my companion. "Everyone has a story."

"Mine is of service; helping people place their orders, giving them an idea of the menu. Sometimes, starting to believe that you can create what you want can be a little intoxicating. But this place is of service because it's familiar. Can't have you out of your mind and out of your depth all at once! But a little confusion can actually be refreshing."

"You're saying that confusion is desirable?" I was already out of my depth.

"Well, let's say mixing things up a little is helpful; it brings a new perspective. But we don't want you shaken; just stirred sufficiently to broaden your horizons. Creating more choice can be confusing... Not everyone knows what they want when the menu changes. They order something else, taste it and then want to change it. You know how it is."

"Yes," I agreed sympathetically. "I'm a bit like that. I've come here not really knowing what's on offer. I'm willing to give it a try, just don't really know what to expect or what I'm getting myself into."

"Nothing has to be what you think it'll be. You're not trying to be your old self, are you? That doesn't work here. If you want my advice, just keep on being yourself; the one right here, right now. The more you understand you, the more you can understand the experience of you. You're open minded, right?"

"I hope so. Ironically, I've been focusing on just that these past few days. It's been both disturbing and liberating. I'm used to knowing what to do and where I am but that doesn't seem to apply here. But I'm glad to be here."

"Yes I understand. And you've been demonstrating your willingness to change; it's all over town. Didn't you hear them speaking to you just then?" asked the voice.

"To be honest, I couldn't actually hear what was being said," I admitted apologetically.

"Never mind, you'll get to meet everyone another time. So what would you like help with? You do want help, don't you?" asked the voice, accent on *help*.

"Oh yes, I do," I said enthusiastically.

"I see. Then, turn your world inside out," came the reply seeming to echo around the room.

"Sorry, I don't understand. What do you mean? Seems a little difficult for a beginner. I was thinking of something a little less obscure. Perhaps 'Go and have lunch at the restaurant on the corner and meet someone who will change your life'—that sort of advice."

"If you want someone else to change your Life or do it for you then, sorry, I can't help."

"Why not?" I demanded with frustration.

"Because it isn't my job. I'm here to provide choice, not tell you what to do. No one can create your experience, it's yours for the making and the experiencing. Why don't you consume what you ordered first and then you can choose something different next time? We cater for all tastes here, it's just that the orders need to be consumed on the premises."

"Yes of course, I understand… in the sense that I know you are trying to help me. But how can I choose if I don't understand the choice?" I replied, perplexed.

"You don't need to know in order to choose, you are required to feel. Turn your world inside out and it'll all make sense. If you want a hint, you can start by changing your mind. Do you believe that you can turn your world inside out?"

"I feel so," I replied, not really understanding what I'd just said.

"We're in agreement then. The rest is just details. Well, it's been lovely. Drop by again soon. You've caused quite a stir… Remember, we're always open." The voice began to fade.

"But I've got more questions. Just how, precisely, am I going to turn my world inside out?" I raised my voice hoping the increased volume would persuade my companion to stay. But there was no reply.

Just two sips from my enormous drink and it was finished. I marveled at how I could drink so little and it amount to so much. Perhaps I did get the perfect measure after all. The room began to blur then my head began to spin.

——— ——— ———

The bathroom door slammed. I opened my eyes with a start. My body was slightly stiff but I felt energized. No meditation hangover for me! I smiled. But wait a minute, perhaps in a way there was, in the form of the phrase 'turn your world inside out' repeating itself over and over again in my head like a mantra.

I looked over at the clock, remembering I had a 1pm lunch appointment with a Delhi contact. It was already 11:11. I was astonished. If I hadn't been asleep, which I was certain I hadn't, where had I been for an hour and a half? Peering into the moments before, I heard an echo of a phrase; 'Turn your world inside out.'

"What on Earth was that?" I asked the walls. There was no reply. I repeated the phrase over and over again, trying to rearrange the words to find an order that made more sense. But there was none and any other hints appeared to have evaporated. I went back to basics.

My first question was, 'Which world am I turning inside out?' The voice felt helpful and encouraging so inside out must be some kind of expansion. Would I gain more expansion by turning Existence inside out? I didn't feel Existence could cope with that amount of flexibility, so it must be turning Life inside out? But I still didn't feel the zing, the truth rush that confirmed my Heart's endorsement. It wasn't so much that this was too simple, it was more a case of too superficial. Discovering the world I was turning inside out required a change of direction.

"Step back," I told myself. "You can't see for looking. Make some space." I closed my eyes and returned to meditation. No sooner had I restarted my 'doing nothingness' than an iridescent balloon floated a message into my silent shade. "Don't look in the same places. And don't look in the same way."

Opening my eyes, I realized I was bouncing between the walls of conditioning. I was rebounding from one extreme of thinking to another. If it wasn't Existence then the answer had to be Life. If it wasn't one side of the coin, it had to be the other. No one ever said there could be other coins with a different number of sides! If I was going to turn my world inside out and keep expanding, perhaps it was going to turn into something completely different.

Perhaps my meditation conversation had given me a view of another world that overlapped and expanded beyond Existence, even beyond Life? What if the world I was turning inside out wasn't black and white, not even grey but a glorious technicolor? Perhaps it was the 'white' at the end of the tunnel that contained all colors, shades and, more importantly, all the answers?

Bingo! I felt a Truth Rush. I named this new inside-out world 'RealLife'. RealLife was a place where creations came only from the Heart and there were no limits; no fear of loss, be it of love, abundance or truth. It was a place where creation never ended, it just kept on flowing. Creating was an experience of a true unending flow; there was continual learning and change; experiences were created, enjoyed and relinquished. In RealLife there was no point, nor inclination, to hold onto anything or anyone because of the fear of losing out. RealLife had no fear, loss or lack, only flow. I felt fulfilled and my new expansion was complete. The inside-out world had flowed into RealLife and I wanted more.

Fact or fiction

As the weeks passed, my meditations merged into one continually lengthening conversation. The conversation stopped when I stopped and started again with perfect continuity when I next settled back into my inner space. The sensations and environments kept changing but without contradicting the previous flow of learning. It was addictive, frustrating, inspiring and puzzling. The length of time I spent made no difference to how much I understood or felt.

The more I questioned these conversations, the more ideas were stimulated. There was no right or wrong answer, just a stream of alternatives. I hadn't actually seen 'the voice' yet. I had countless impressions but never a face. And yet talking to a presence rather than a form was no less real. All the qualities of a normal conversation were there, just no other person. What was better than normal conversation was the absence of conflict, condescension and feeling ignorant or inadequate. We never argued, just clarified. The voice didn't try to convince me of anything nor did it judge my replies and comments. It was the best listening I'd ever heard.

Still, my mind, when it could get a word in edge ways, persisted in lecturing me on my undoing, wrestling with my illogical explorations and supposed lack of productivity. "What are you doing wasting your time? You've come to write a travel book, not sit in your apartment and go nowhere. Why are you looking into things you know nothing about and you don't understand? This isn't your area. Stay with what you know. If you've got a question, just ask an expert, someone who is qualified, just like you've always done. Face the facts, it's that simple."

But I was rebelling. By now RealLife had shown me that this kind of explanation simply wasn't enough. The facts of the mind were superficial limits far from the simple wisdoms I was seeking.

Facts were products of perceptions from within Existence. The road of factuality was leading us away from discovering what we really believed, in favor of letting external authorities make our choices for us. Why waste time and effort discovering our own perceptions? There were experts in Existence to do that for us. There was no point in implementing our own perspectives, it was simply a waste of time. Facts had done all the work for us. They'd become the backbone of Existence, defining what we could and couldn't do, assuming they could protect us from the danger of the unknown.

But what if we didn't perceive the unknown to be dangerous? We didn't have to get stuck in the ever-tightening fear fabric of Existence. What if assumed danger was the single most common barrier that Existence had put between us and Life?

I was beginning to understand why the voice had said that there was no point in telling me what to do. It had no interest in becoming my external authority or making me dependent. There was no expansion in that, just more Existence. What the voice wanted to do was help me feel and become aware my own perspectives and perceptions. Expansion meant understanding how I felt about my experience, and I was the only one qualified for the job.

If I looked at the facts of life, they were few and invariably far between. Life had many more relativities and uncertainties. In the fabric of Life, factuality was only one thread in amongst a continual pattern of truth. There was a liberating lack of definition in Life because Life was designed to embrace, not alienate. We could all travel through our own patterning and still our individual threads of truth would meet at a common point. There was no fine line between right and wrong, but there was insight.

Insight could happen in Life because experience was 'in sight' instead of being veiled by external authorities. Insight in Existence was like wearing someone else's glasses and being unable to see anything clearly. True insight could never be achieved through the opinions of another. In Life, each individual had the capacity to develop and alter their own perception as their vision and wisdom developed. The greater the insight, the greater the ability to change the mind and the experience.

I considered the changing truths of the past three weeks. Meditation was no longer 'doing nothing', it was simply different; an alternative something that wasn't made up exclusively of doing. I didn't have to 'do' to make progress. Progress wasn't just an outwardly directed action. It could be an inward expansion with no specific direction or subject. I was getting somewhere, just without knowing exactly where that somewhere was.

Meditation was a going-with-the-flow, a progress that wasn't rational but all the same was useful. I'd spent time in a place that had no time, had conversations with someone I'd never met and learnt more about myself than all the learned logic I'd accumulated previously. I was feeling the flow of Life rather than using all my energy to make the unknown rational. No more analyzing until my world fell into meaningless pieces. I was inspired to discover rather than assume or define. Like an astronaut in outer space, I was changing my world simply by changing my perspective each time I returned o Earth.

Perhaps meditation was the answer to 'Is there anybody out there?'; the 'contact' that many longed for; an interdimensional portal that allowed interaction out of time and three dimensional space. Facts told me this wasn't possible. Nothing existed on any other neighboring planets; there simply wasn't anyone there to contact. But being in Life opened up the possibility of other truths.

What if those on other worlds spent their time on inner journeys of being, leaving no trace of the structures they had built? What if those on Earth responsible for searching for Life were looking in a different place or on a different wavelength that the rest of our neighbors didn't use?

What if, sadly, the rest of our solar system had seen what we'd done to our own planet and considered us so primitive and destructive that we simply weren't worth contact? Perhaps the fact of our matter was that we were the least evolved, the real aliens of our star system, separating ourselves through a destructive control instead of a free flowing harmony. It was we who couldn't sustain contact because we couldn't sustain the alternatives required to enable it.

Maybe meditation was one of those alternative avenues, filling the gap between our worlds. Instead of asking "Is there anybody out there?", perhaps it was a better idea to ask "Is there anybody in here?"

Becoming the job

The setting sun confirmed the end of the day's truth trail as the warm red glow surrendered to its nightly rebirth. An escort of urban eagles ushered in the dusk and I relaxed back into my chair with a sense of purpose and a twilight vision of a unified landscape where Existence, Life and RealLife merged into one before me. The road through Existence was a single lane highway with a permanent speed limit and routine for transport. Life was a multilane highway with vehicles of choice, varying speeds and directions. RealLife was a freeway with no limits that flowed with the natural landscape, never conflicting or constricting, simply unfolding.

I drifted through leafy lanes and congested cities. I began to fly above the flashing neons, over desolate mountain ranges and remote forests.

The demanding tones of the telephone brought me crashing through a tropical canopy and back into the room. I took a few seconds to come to my physical senses and picked up the receiver. It was my editor calling from London.

"Yes, it's Erica here. How are you? And how's the new book coming along?" she asked in gushing expectancy.

"To be honest, it's a bit bogged at present, Erica." I paused, still sounding a little dazed. "The monsoon is making traveling really difficult so I decided to spend this month planning rather than struggling against the elements. Some of the places I wanted to include don't even feature on regular maps. It takes some thought. You know how it is." I was fudging and she knew it.

"Well, wouldn't be much of an editor if I didn't know how it was." She paused, still curious. "So what have you been doing with yourself?" she continued, as if peering down the telephone to check on the pile of scribbled pages on my desk.

"Researching about the journey of course. Just haven't been out much, that's all. I needed to get the overall picture, not just bits. The facts in India are just a departure point; there's always more to it. If there's one thing I've learnt this past month, it's that things are never what they seem."

"Okay, give us a call when the 'being' and the 'seeming' synchronize. You'll be glad to know, I also called to tell you that the deadline has been put back a month, so that should help your 'rain stop play'."

"Spoken like a true cricket devotee. You'd fit in fine here Erica. Thanks for telling me," I replied, trying to hide my relief.

"Well, I'll call you when things are beginning to take shape," I said reassuringly.

"Fine. Enjoy your Indian summer." The line clicked and she was gone.

I settled back into my chair, closed my eyes and continued peering into my inner landscape. As I scanned the horizon of Existence I saw all shapes and forms interspersed with green islands and blue oases. The buildings were arranged in a regimented intensity, competing for space and standing in some sort of physical hierarchy. The land gave off an aura of tightness and claustrophobia. I could feel myself being sucked in between the skyscrapers. Before I knew it I was in a taxi in the middle of rush hour, squeezing through narrow lanes of congested traffic at break neck speed.

"Slow down," I shouted, and the driver slammed on his brakes, skidding to a stop, narrowly missing the car in front.

"What on Earth are you doing?! You nearly hit the vehicle in front!" I reacted hysterically.

"It's a joy ride. Relax. This is how it's got to be in the rush hour — rush or be rushed; see a space and fill it," replied the driver casually as if there was nothing out of the ordinary.

"This is no joy ride, it's an adrenalin trip! I'm getting out."

"You won't get anything different lady. This is how it is at this time—drive yourself or be driven," replied the driver, shaking his head.

"Well, if that's the case, I'd rather walk," I fumed giving the driver his fare. Opening the car door, I saw a narrow corridor of opportunity. I took it. The rush hour parted and I took one giant step across the pavement and through the double doors into a bar and restaurant called Heaven Can Wait.

My head was pounding and my feet throbbing. I headed straight to the bar and sat down as soon as I was able. A shiver of pent up stress went straight through my body. Chilled by adrenaline and vowing I'd never get in any more taxis, I slumped on the bar as if I was already drunk.

"Your usual?" said a familiar voice from inside the fridge.

"I don't know what I want at the moment," I gasped. "I'll just settle for peace of mind, right now."

"Please do. No hurry. You've got all the time in this world," replied the voice, closing the fridge and writing numbers on an order form.

"You could have fooled me," I replied.

"Well, from time to time that can happen," replied the barman turning around to face me.

"Don't I know you?" I asked. "You sound really familiar."

"Yes, we've met before but not in this place. Still, a change is as good as a rest. So what can I get you?"

"Some answers would be good. Who was that driver? Nearly drained all of the life out of me."

"Oh, that was Ego. Doesn't like taking no for an answer. Has very rigid ideas. Thinks he knows what you want. Only problem is, it's always what he wants. It's all about him, you see." The barman continued polishing the glasses.

"Well, I don't want to be driven by Ego, that's for sure," I replied emphatically.

"So, what *do* you want?"

"Some water. I feel really dizzy. Have I got the energetic Bends? Descending down into this and then rushing here… everything has become so distorted. Am I rambling?" I said apologetically.

"No, carry on," replied the barman patiently.

"Well, where is here? It's not the same 'here' as last time."

"No, this is the link between Existence and Life; the slip road. Part of you has accelerated onto to it, hence the temporary plunge and now the rebound. You're becoming aware of your research."

"What research? I don't remember anything about research."

"Well, most researchers never do. But if you hadn't become aware, we wouldn't be having this conversation. You're just a bit shaken up, scattered. There are parts of you in Existence, parts of you in Life and parts of you in RealLife. You've been researching the worlds within worlds ever since you turned your world inside out. So congratulations!" exclaimed the barman, putting a large glass of water directly in front of me. I gulped down the water until it poured out the side of my mouth.

"You really are thirsty! Another one?"

"Absolutely."

"Coming right up."

Suddenly I felt completely refreshed, launching into a flow of questions.

"So, I am researching experience here in Existence, right now?"

"Yes. It's the first place on your map," confirmed the barman. "Your innocence brought you."

"But how could that have happened? If I'm innocent, I wouldn't know anything about this place, far less choose it. I'd be ignorant, naïve. I don't understand how the two are connected."

"Well, that definition is one from within Existence but it

doesn't necessarily apply anywhere else. For example, that statement isn't true in Life. What you know in Life isn't what you know in Existence."

"This is a learning vertical and you're just about to lose me. Can you slow down?"

"Certainly. Innocence is really your Inner Sense. This became limited in Existence so the complete meaning isn't obvious to you. It's your Inner Sense that brought you here so you could discover this place in a new Light. Now you're looking *into* Existence rather than looking *from* within it."

"So I'm getting the overview of a researcher; becoming more objective about Existence, thanks to my Inner-Sense? I might be naïve about Life but I've had plenty of experience in Existence."

"Yes, exactly. Now you're able to put your experience of Existence into context; seeing the difference between research here, in Life, and in RealLife. When Ego said 'Driving this way is the only way', you didn't settle for his extremes. You consulted your Inner Sense and sought an alternative. You looked outside the limited view.

"The trick to being here while researching is to not lose your Inner Sense. If you do, all your research into Limitation, such as fear and lack, will become the only knowledge you register. So instead of doing the job, you'll become the job. Most in Existence don't know what they know. They've forgotten what true knowledge is and have substituted it for Ego opinions and facts. They're forgetting that they came only to stay for a while to look into Limitation, not to get caught up in it and move in permanently."

"Well, after today there's no fear of that. I couldn't be persuaded to stay here," I said decidedly.

"Don't be so sure of that. Ego can be very persuasive. In this phase of your research, you've accelerated onto the slip road between Existence and Life. However, there are still parts of you content to remain within Existence. That's why it's called the slip road! Enough of you can still slip back into Existence."

"So I'm glad I didn't get the shock of my life for no reason," I laughed nervously.

"Well, it was a necessary part of your learning. In acceleration you get an intense experience of the fear you are leaving behind. You've had a shock introduction, but that can be all too attractive."

"Now I'm really confused. There is no way I would choose to repeat that taxi ride. I am absolutely certain about that."

"No of course not. But ironically, the 'never-say-never-again' syndrome can be all it takes to keep you here. Remember, you're collecting research, not accumulating likes and dislikes. The stronger you resist, possess or obsess, the more magnetized you become to Existence. Strong likes and dislikes can be all it takes to get stuck here."

"So no huge mood swings then. Out with hype, in with harmony," I added quickly.

"Yes. Keep it light and don't get attached to outcomes or make dramas out of perceived crises. This is the greatest show on Earth but you don't have to leave the audience. Ego can be brash but he is also a fantastic entertainer. Be it subtlety, sympathy or tragedy, Ego is always sending out hooks to catch you in endless complication and mental mazes. One hook is all it takes. Remember, Ego is always your biggest fan. This is why Limitation has such a draw. Ego will juggle any amount of experiences to gain more and more attention. With each reaction, you become more and more unconscious of your doing and being. Before you know it, you'll be hooked, the web of highs and lows ensuring you become missing in action."

"So today's research was polarized—a big enough contrast so that I could practice using my Inner Sense? Get my capability up to speed without getting hooked?"

"Yes, an introduction. Please don't misunderstand me, there's nothing wrong with Ego. Limitation wouldn't be possible without Ego. He's the perfect man for the job but he can easily recruit you to work for him. The more you do, the more you will exchange choice for control, expansion for Limitation until Ego, not you, runs your experience. Just remember, nothing is real and everything can change."

"So what happens to those who don't listen and become the job?"

"Well, when a researcher becomes strongly attached to Existence, it becomes harder and harder to research anywhere else. If the researcher still wants to move on from Existence, a huge adjustment is required to create an alternative view. Ego will never leave you; only you can choose to move out of Existence and leave Ego."

"So do you mean the person creates a kind of wake up call?"

"Yes. The greater the hooks in Existence, the greater the gap between the part of the researcher in Existence and, in turn, in Life and in RealLife. The greater the potential difference between Life and Existence, the greater the spark! If most of the researcher is Existing, you can imagine the shock to bring them back into balance."

The barman paused, put my glass in the sink and began drawing on the bar mat. Pointing to his would-be blackboard he continued;

"Remember your serviette in the coffee shop? Well, here's an update." He drew three intersecting circles on a bar mat. The left hand circle he marked E, the middle circle P and the last circle to the right he labeled M.

"This is your mental body, the area that organizes. It's your ability to think; your mind; your worries and analyses," he said pointing to the circle M furthest to the right. "This central circle is your physical presence, your body. Call it your physicality.

This circle on the left is your Emotional body where all of your emotional reactions, responses and memories are stored."

I looked carefully at what he had drawn.

"So if I understand this correctly," I began; "when the three circles overlap, the person is within the three aspects. They feel a bit, think a bit and are physically present. The energy of the person is distributed within these three areas in varying proportions. Say, if all the circles were superimposed, then the person would be completely balanced because all of the circles would be united together in a type of 3D harmony?" I felt I was beginning to understand the concepts.

"Yes. The person's intention, action and feeling would be completely unified. They would be living a completely Heart-centered life."

"But we don't often perceive balance as useful in Existence, right?"

"No. It's a pretty under-valued state of being."

"So if we give up responsibility for our life, we look to Ego to take more and more control."

"Yep."

"And if Ego's headquarters is in the mind then our world becomes a mind-centered one rather than a Heart-centered one."

"Absolutely. This is why in Existence it's easy to see how people concentrate more and more of their energy in their mind until their Ego is really holding them hostage in the mental circle, here." He pointed to the right hand circle. "Free thinking is gone and Ego takes over all their decisions. The more you try to protect yourself from the fear of change, the more you move into the future and away from your emotionality and physicality. In the extreme case, your mental body comes adrift, separate and isolated from your physical and emotional centers. The greater the gap, the greater the imbalance and the greater the event required to get back into balance. The body cannot exist without the mind, so if there is any part of the person still in Life, it's time to choose a Wake Up Call.

"So Operation Wake Up Call is designed to bring the person back into some kind of balance and release them from the prison of the mind?"

"Yes," replied the barman, "and this can happen at either end of the scale."

"I see so what you're saying is one end of the scale is the anger, and control of existing with Ego only in the mind and the other end of the scale is existing in emotional disharmony in the emotional body, always holding on to the past, regretting, feeling guilt, obsessing about what could have happened instead of what is happening now."

"Exactly. The disconnection can also happen when the Ego isolates the person in the Emotional circle and they exist in an unending drama of what could have been and or the emotional hurt they believe they cannot release."

"So again, if there is any of the person remaining in Life they will create another wake up call to get reconnected with their physical and mental selves."

"Quite right" said the barman. "Be it a near miss, a heart attack or a profound depression, it's chosen by the researcher to put Existence on mute, to hear the subtle tones of their Inner Sense and come full circle so they can return to balance."

Going with the flow

"Well, that's it for today." The barman smiled.

"What a shame. This discussion is so helpful. I really thought we were getting somewhere."

"We are! Just not the same place! I'm off, it's the end of my shift."

"So, time to stop serving advice?"

"Just time to serve myself a break. You won't get bored here; there is plenty to quench your appetite for exploration."

"Thanks for all the explanations. It makes perfect sense and I really appreciate it. Great to finally get to know you better. Everything was such a blur before."

"Less focused, perhaps. You've got more clarity now. This place isn't so bad, right?"

"No, I'm really enjoying it, now I've adjusted. I'll explore a bit more, stay a while longer. Or is there a time limit here?"

"Well, there are lots of limits as you can feel. But as always, it's whether you believe the external authority or your own. Being here is part of your journey and that's always changing. So enjoy your experience rather than the time it takes to accumulate it."

"Great. More research then?"

"Yes. But before I go, you'll probably require a map."

"Is it a map of the secret tunnel between Existence and Life?"

"No. A street map showing you the less-than-secret way to get from A to B," said the barman, unfolding a tourist map.

"You are here. There's lots of entertainment along this strip. Two traffic lights down there's a great bookshop on the corner if you want a change of scene."

"Great. Everything appears to be in walking distance. No need for cabs!"

"Yes, you're right. But there's nothing wrong with the cabs, it's just your reaction to them that you need to be aware of."

"Oh that's right—no cab drivers from hell, just contrast and choice."

Nodding, the barman took his rucksack from under the bar, shouted a greeting to his colleague, and left.

'Well no use sitting here… time to explore, gather research.'

Merging with the busy foot traffic, I found myself at the

next intersection in double quick time. I stopped to window shop and then remembered the map. I took it out to see if I was going in the right direction for the bookshop. I wasn't.

Turning around, I started to walk back the way I'd come, becoming overwhelmed by the sensation that I was going in the wrong direction. People bumped into me as if unable or unwilling to register my presence. I began to feel defensive, estranged from an unconscious environment. My pace quickened as my frustration began to surface. I caught a glimpse of my driven face in the window of a children's clothes shop. Then, when I looked back again, I was face to face with a huge poster of an exotic holiday getaway.

I moved off the teeming thoroughfare and stared into the travel agent's window. I wondered whether, if I focused long enough, I could transport myself onto the beach, diving into the waves and smelling the sea air. I waited... but nothing happened, no matter how hard I tried to transport myself.

"Your learning is here. No environment will change that," I heard someone say in my left ear. "Resistance will only alienate you further so surrender; go with the flow. You'll be where you want to be soon enough, just not the way you planned. Relax. Adapt. If you don't react then the limitation you are experiencing will cease to exist. You're researching your environment, not becoming it. Don't try and change Limitation, change your response to it..."

I turned around expecting to see the barman standing behind me but there was no one, just the voice. I rejoined the crush of people and left my defensive attitude sunbathing on the beach. As I arrived at the traffic lights I saw the bookshop. It was closed. In the same moment the lights changed and the green man beckoned me over the road. I looked across the intersection to see another Heaven Can Wait bar and restaurant. 'This must be Existence's most successful franchise,' I smiled to myself, walking down the steps to the restaurant.

The Bar of Conditioning

As soon as I entered the bar, my expectations began to dissolve. Instead of the quiet casual atmosphere of the first Heaven Can Wait, this bar was full to capacity. The atmosphere was smoky, charged with perfume, adrenalin and singletons.

My feet stuck to the beer-soaked carpet as I tried to get a snack menu. Progress from the entrance to the main bar was slow with clumps of chairs and tables springing up everywhere, bordered by secluded alcoves with 'Members Only' signs. There was a sea of faces displaying every expression I could ever remember seeing in Existence. Everyone looked like someone I used to know, just about to approach me for that 'long time, no see' drink and catch-up chat.

A couple in smart business attire waved to me from a Members table. I surrendered to my lack of progress and drifted towards the visual invitation.

"How are you?" said the man standing up to greet me with a firm handshake while his partner moved around the booth in a welcoming gesture, making room for me to sit down. "Where have you been hiding these past weeks? Join us and tell us what you've been up to," he continued enthusiastically.

"Sorry, my memory's really bad these days. I know I know you but, you know how it is… so many names, so few matching faces."

"It's John and Sophie," replied the man, a little taken aback. "You remember us from the publishing awards last month? Charlton Inc; only the sixth biggest global now, after the merger."

"Oh yes, of course," I said sitting down. "How stupid of me. How's it been going?"

"To be frank, terrible. We've just had the worst figures in five years. There's talk of yet another merger. We're hoping it'll only affect middle management and below."

"What about looking for another job; branch out; start your own company?"

"Oh, no point in that. It's all about the top ten now. Rather be a big fish in a small pond than the other way around. It's the market trend—go with a tried and tested; that's where the security is. No room for risk, the market doesn't support it. If you fit in then you can get some security, make things a bit more predictable. I'm too old to start out on my own; that's simply not an option. Know so many people who've tried to do it and they always come back. But then they have to take a pay cut, go a lot lower down the ladder."

"But surely there's no point in being in the job if you're miserable. Perhaps you can take your editing skills and apply them to a different product- newspapers, magazines?"

"Oh no, too specialized. When you come up to forty it's simply too risky to change. You need years and years of experience and that's something I don't have. Still, everyone's in the same boat. Let's face it, who ever really gets a job they love? It's just about earning money, keeping going. Loving what you do is just something that people who can't commit make up so they can cover up their lack of responsibility. There's no point in bucking the system, it's the security in life."

I found it hard to stay awake in the face of such relentless justification of struggle and professional victimhood. I drained my glass and, as my wellbeing didn't appear to be far behind, I sought a break in the black cloud downpour to make my get away.

"Fancy another drink?" asked Sophie.

"No, I'll pass. Thanks anyway."

Smiling and wishing John and Sophie the very best in their destiny of doom, I left the table. Walking slowly towards the bar, I realized they were researchers who'd become completely resigned to being the job. They embraced Limitation to the best of their ability. There weren't any alternatives for them. They weren't getting a life, they were rejecting it. They saw those who deviated as Peter Pans who didn't want the responsibilities of a serious life; caught in a dream world, floating in clouds of joy and fulfillment.

My hunger for food and alternative company propelled me to the bar and I asked for the snacks menu with a hypoglycemic edge, my coat brushing the person seated next to me.

"Sorry," I said clumsily.

"No problem. All part of the hub. It's busy tonight." he commented, striking up conversation. "Can I get you a drink?"

"Kind of you to ask but I really want some food," I said, scanning the menu.

"Okay, how about a vodka martini and a salmon salad? The food's great here."

"Wonderful. Thanks." I was taken aback by such spontaneous generosity.

"My pleasure. If you don't mind me saying, it looks like you haven't eaten for days."

"Well, it's not that long, but you're right, I am starving. Are you waiting for someone?"

"Yes and no. My date cancelled but I have another friend who said they might meet me here around 6:30 so I'm waiting for their text."

"Why don't you text them?"

"I could I suppose, but I think they're still in a meeting, so I'll wait."

"You don't know if you don't try. You might be waiting all night," I continued.

"Yes, you're right, of course. What do you do?" he asked, changing the subject.

"I'm a researcher. I'm researching a new book."

"Oh that sounds interesting. What's it about?"

"That's a very good question. It's a work in progress. I'm

not quite sure where it's going yet, but fundamentally it's about the choice to change; change your mind and recycle your fears into your dreams; create the life you want instead of settling for what others think you should do or be. It's a philosophical journey based in India."

"Sounds great. India seems such a spiritual place. Always wanted to trip out in Goa but haven't been yet. I've been thinking about change but with so much going on, it never quite seems to be the right time. How do you know when it's a good time to change? So it'll work out, I mean?"

"Well, it's always a good time. All you require is a little TLC," I said optimistically.

"What? Tender loving care?" he replied.

"No. Trust, Love and Courage. Trust that 'out there'," I said, gesturing towards the dance floor, "will help you. Love and put your Heart into what you've chosen and have the Courage to take the plunge. When you get out the other side of change, it's never as bad or difficult as it first appeared."

"I hear what you're saying," he said. "Just the other day my work colleague was saying I should get a better job, stretch my limits, shop around. I'm open to it, just the trouble is, how do you know you're making the right decision?..."Oh, that's my phone. One moment," he said, turning away to answer the call.

I turned back to the bar just in time to see a second round of drinks.

"I didn't order anything else," I said, turning back to my companion. But he had left.

"Your friend apologizes. He had to leave. The drink's on the house; a gift from your friend behind the bar," said the waiter.

I was surprised. "Who's that?" I asked, raising my voice above the music.

"Michael. He's serving the lady at the end of the bar," replied the waiter.

"Oh, *that* Michael," I said, with no idea who he was

talking about. "Thanks. Can you tell him I'd like a chance to thank him when he's got a minute."

"Of course. I'll ask him to come over before he goes on his break."

Finding an exit

Within a few minutes I saw a man I now recognized to be Michael smiling his way in my direction.
"Thanks for the drink. I didn't know your name was Michael, and that when you said 'later' you meant this soon!"

"Well, when you're researching consciously, everything comes around just that bit quicker. Call it a kind of acceleration. How are you enjoying this Heaven Can Wait?"

"It's certainly an experience; very different to the other bar. Not great for research because I can't hear myself feel or think. Is there anywhere else we can talk?"

"What about the staff lounge out back?"

"Great."

We went through a door marked 'Staff Only' and into a small room with two sofas, a coffee machine and stacks of plastic chairs. The club pulsed through the adjoining wall.

"So how's your night going?" asked Michael.

"Well, it's really curious; full of memories and glimpses of people I thought I knew but I simply don't remember. My mind doesn't seem to want to access the past. It's as if it's been wiped."

"So what does it feel like to have near memories?"

"Fine," I replied. "Before, in Existence, I used to fill photo albums with special occasions, holidays and celebrations, but now the need to hold on to all that has gone. This place is great but transitory; I don't feel it's somewhere I would like to return. If you said to me 'Let's leave now' I wouldn't hesitate. There's nothing wrong, I'm not compelled to leave, but if you suggested somewhere else, I would choose to leave."

"Well, I'm on a break now. Want to get a breath of fresh air?"

"Fine. Is that the exit over there?"

"Yes. After you," replied Michael with an old fashioned flare.

I pushed open the door, expecting to be greeted by a night sky contrasted with bright neons… but the city had vanished. I was standing knee deep in lavender with the sun directly overhead. I collapsed into clouds of scent and began to laugh hysterically.

"How did we get here?" I spluttered.

Michael sat down beside me. "You got here by getting out of your own way."

"So… that would mean I let go of the fear of moving forward by coming here."

"In a way. Also, you were prepared to embrace an honest appraisal of what you now want as opposed to what you did want. The old you is no longer standing in the way of the new you."

"So I would be standing in my own way when I'm resisting being true to me, when I'm limiting myself through the fear of what might be or what I might lose?"

"Yes."

"So when I was resisting the flow of Existence, when I didn't like the taxi driver, the crush of people, I couldn't accelerate anywhere. That's why I couldn't get to the beach?"

"Yes."

"But now I'm aware of my research, I can move differently, benefit from the acceleration that a change of scene brings?"

"Yes."

"Are you going to say anything but 'yes'?"

"Yes."

"Ha ha! So where are we now?"

"You're the one with all the realizations. You tell me," replied Michael.

"Inspiration-harvesting," I answered decidedly.

"What field of inspiration?" Michael moved further.

"Well, it isn't Existence, of that I'm certain. But it doesn't feel like Life either. We're resting somewhere in between, out of time and out of hassle."

"Okay. So what would you like to ask me while we enjoy our between world?"

"Can I ask you about the club, Heaven Can Wait?"

"Absolutely."

"Who runs it and what does it really represent?"

"The Club is a concentrated version of your Ego conditioning. It's run mostly by your Ego but there are also other influences. It's the Bar of Conditioning, where everything finds its level. The Club gave you the chance to play out the most accessible layers of your own conditioning. You came, you saw, and you left behind the layers of conditioning you didn't want anymore. You ceased to allow those layers to define who you are. You stopped relying on your Ego for a good time and began to take responsibility for your own joy. You've realized that your fulfillment is somewhere else now.

"As I mentioned before, there is nothing wrong with the Club, it is now that the conditioning that was within it is no longer relevant. As a result, the Club is redundant as a research environment. You've learnt all you can learn from being there."

"So this letting go of conditioning could have happened anywhere?" I added.

"Yes. The location of your realization could have been anywhere. It just so happens that the club was the most user friendly vehicle to get you here. But the learning structure could have been anything. In Existence, Ego is everywhere;

your constant companion and controller—taxi driver, zoo keeper, friend, politician to name but a few. There's an Ego inside every individual born within Existence. Without Ego there wouldn't be any separation, any contrast between Existence and Life, between Love and Fear, Expansion and Limitation. Ego creates limits and has been essential for your research in Limitation. You couldn't have achieved what you've achieved without Ego."

"But what about you? You're different. Where do you fit in all of this?"

"My origin isn't from within Existence. I'm not a researcher, I'm a guide."

"So you are able to come and go between worlds?"

"Yes, that's my job. I help conduct the traffic between Existence, Life and RealLife. Currently we are parked between Existence and Life, fuelling up with the realizations that will bring you your next acceleration forward."

"So getting out of my own way really means choosing not to consult Ego about my choices?"

"More a case of not letting Ego block who you want to become. Instead of persisting with a head-to-head that you can't win and that just drains your energy, you've stepped aside; created an alternative. Your Ego is still there, it's just that you're making it redundant, step by step. The more of you that leaves Existence, the more of you will be in Life and beyond."

"So previously I used conditioning to shield me from Life and change?"

"Yes. In Existence, Ego tells you that conditioning is the way of Wisdom; that everything you need to know about your experience you can formulate from your conditioning. Of course, this is Ego reinforcing itself. If you make all your choices from Ego, you will simply create more Ego.

He continued, "Think of yourself in a bunker made of your conditioning. You are protected from learning and

Life, seemingly safe in the familiar fears of your Existence. Ego continually tells you about imaginary aggressors and conflicts that kept you controlled. The noises and sensations are very convincing so you allow your Ego to fight this war on your behalf. Until one day you wake up and realize you are in a one man war with your Ego. When you finally poke your head above the bunker and decide to come out, there is no war, no assault and no real danger. Ego has disappeared, too cowardly to face you, so there is nothing between you and your walk to freedom. That is, nothing except your choice to move forward."

"So my personal war is over now because I've surrendered my conditioning and stopped believing in my Ego?"

"Yes, in part. There are still areas of you that are conditioning-driven, but you've made your major breakthrough. Ego will still try and fight you but as long as you dismantle more conditioning and remain peaceful, Ego will never confine you to Existence again. As you become more aware you will recognize what you are required to let go. Ego will be less and less capable of threatening you."

"So conditioning is like a stockpile of Ego weapons, but they are useless when we aren't afraid of being without them."

"Exactly. You can now see that conditioning isn't a set of rules that is vital to sustain life. Nor is it a sophisticated array of weapons with which to defend yourself. It's a selection of limits that your Ego thinks are essential to keep you under control. Now you've won one of the most important battles within yourself, you aren't afraid of Existence becoming worse nor do you see it as the only way to be. You've got a Life now. Procrastination, doubt and denial can become part of your past... if you let them."

Passing the point of no return

I was now feeling more relaxed. Michael understood what I was thinking and was helping me discover what I was feeling. Before, all I'd allow to support me were facts and what I thought I knew. Now I had someone with whom I could discuss the difference.

"So, to keep your awareness and center in Life, it's helpful to study Ego?" I continued.

"Indeed," encouraged Michael. "Use the tool of self enquiry as much as you can so Ego becomes obvious to you. There's no reason to fear Ego but remember that parts of you are still in Existence. Just because you place your awareness in Life and beyond doesn't mean that your Ego ceases to influence you. In Heaven Can Wait, you had obvious examples of what you were choosing to leave behind."

"Do you mean the 'we-can't-change-anything' couple?"

"Yes. And more importantly, the fact that this couple *didn't want* to change anything. Those are Existors—ones who see their conditioning as a comfortable place which they are happy to reinforce with all their creativity. They enjoy pure immersion in Limitation. Why do you think it was so draining to be in their company?"

"Because they were so negative."

"Yes, in a way. But you don't have to be an Existor to be negative. Negativity is simply a form of resistance. The degree of the negativity is directly related to how resistant the person is. The more negative someone is, the more they are trying to stay in Existence and resist change. What makes you different to an Existor now is that you don't choose to continue your victimhood; you don't choose to confine the awareness of yourself to your Ego. What about your friend at the bar? Was he an Existor?"

"No. Our conversations felt very different. He appeared open minded and open to change. Didn't seem to have actually got around to what he had planned but at least he wanted to change."

"In Heaven Can Wait, there are plenty of Wannabees, Gonnabees and If-Onlys. Like you, they've recognized the opportunity to expand their horizons, go further afield — even to this place. But why aren't they here?"

"Because they can't make up their minds?" I suggested.

"Yes. Ego is still running their minds, creating endless labyrinths of self denial, procrastination and inability to commit."

"So what's their game?"

"Think of them as a potential athlete — a high jumper for example. They've thought about their event, even trained for it, but they haven't taken their training beyond the mind. Their only barrier is the Bar of Conditioning. All they have to do is get over it.

They run up to their limit but stop at the last minute to see how high it is. Preparing again for another attempt, they stop because they think their technique isn't good enough. After that, they think it isn't the right time. And so it goes on. They allow Ego to pull them back into an Existor mindset when their awareness is just about to spring free."

"So it wasn't enough for me to sit in the Bar of Conditioning. It was also important to talk through it, meet what I was about to let go of and decide to move on. You could say it was 'one-for-the-road' to see if my Ego would keep me there?"

"Yes. You never really know whether you can do without Ego until you do without it. The practical is always full of more surprises," replied Michael.

"So everything's different now, right?"

"Yes, everything." He paused. "Do you want to go for a walk? Say, up to the top of the hill?"

"I'd love to."

When we reached the top of the hill, the landscape was

lavender in all directions as far as the eye could see except for a dark circle a couple of miles away to the west.

"What's that?" I asked pointing to the dark form.

"Oh, that's what you left behind. It represents the Club and your Bar of Conditioning."

I felt a wave of grief blow through me like a sudden gust of wind.

"Feeling sad?" asked Michael.

"A little, perhaps. It's Ego nostalgia, but there's no desire to go back now. I had great times when I was in Existence, but that was when I didn't know about alternatives. How ironic that such a small dot on the landscape could have kept me entertained for so long!" A few tears fell from my cheeks onto the flowers, turning them magenta on contact.

I stepped back in amazement. "What's that?"

"The flow of change. Magenta is that colour. The vibration that dissolves any residual resistance you have to becoming aware of your Life. This is a choice-enriched environment. It responds to you instantaneously. Your inspiration-harvesting has helped dissolve rigidities of the mind. Now there are fewer dead-ends and sharp edges in the corridors of your mind. Out with the cubes and in with the curves."

"That should help me see around corners," I joked.

"Well, it will help you apply what you've learnt, and start bending a few limits."

"Strange to be grieving for something I no longer want."

"Indeed, but nothing is ever what it seems. It's all part of the researcher's job description."

"Okay, I'm ready," I said, turning back to look at Michael. "Where to next?"

"Back to school," replied Michael with a huge grin.

I winced. "You mean a classroom? Teacher? Note taking?"

"Yep."

"But what's the point of that? I thought we'd established

that facts don't embrace the truth. Well, not the whole truth and nothing but the truth."

"This is a different school. It isn't in Existence," replied Michael.

"So what's the subject? Truth?"

"Actually, 'The Truth, the whole Truth and nothing but the Truth' would be too much for one lesson so all you're going to do is re-learn learning; make some space; clear some of that mental clutter; discover what you really want to learn instead of what you think you know. The difference can be very subtle but its implications can be life changing."

"Okay. Re-learning learning. Where are we going to do that?" I surrendered to the thought that I was revisiting some of the worst years of my Existence.

"Relax. Surrender. Take a rest after your uphill climb."

I sat amongst the lavender and scooped up handfuls of scent. Michael continued talking but the words became heavier and heavier until my body was completely relaxed and my eyelids were closed. I lay down in a sea of blur and was soon drifting higher and higher on thermals of purple.

Back to school

I awoke suddenly to a sharp dig in the ribs. "What's the matter with you? Didn't you sleep last night?" said the verbal jibe seated next to me.

"Obviously not," I replied, lifting my head and regaining my focus.

"Well, you'd better pay attention because there's going to be a practical soon. I can't always bail you out of chemistry, you know!"

In a flash I knew it was pointless saying 'You know me? We're in chemistry?', so I was quiet. I'd come to re-learn learning and knowing nothing was a good place to start.

"So what's the practical about?" I asked, risking my ignorance.

"The Alchemy Of Change, of course. Did you lose some brain cells in your snooze?"

"No. Just checking" I said, laughing off my internal panic.

"Shoosh. Mr Baxter is starting the three R's now."

"Those being?" I thought it better to clarify rather than assume.

"Response, Rejoicement and Relinquishment. That's it, I'm starting a list. I'm adding not- knowing-whether-you're-coming-or-going to memory loss. Or have you forgotten that already too?"

"No, but those aren't the three R's I learnt," I protested while trying to keep my voice down.

"Now that's a first. This is a new subject and you're asleep all the time, plus you've already learnt it. What a laugh. Have you developed sleep learning?"

"Yes!... Only joking. The last laugh is on me, I assure you. Don't worry, I thought I had learnt this but I haven't; it's all new. We'd better shut up." Just as I'd finished, Mr Baxter threw a piercing glance in our direction.

"Do you have something to share, you two at the back?"

We both clamped our jaws and shook our heads.

"I'll take that as a no. Well, as I was saying… The Alchemy Of Change is founded on choice, commitment to change and embracing the learning that unfolds through the cycles of experience. The phases are the choice to experience, the joy of the experience itself, and the letting go of the experience once the learning is completed. When you are balanced and aware, your experience is smooth, you move from each part of the cycle gathering research, gaining Enerjewels, and distilling wisdom. The smoothness of your path forward and the ease in gathering your research is directly proportional to the degree to which you allow Ego and resistance to influence your progress. Ego will always try and interrupt your commitment to change and stop you acquiring Enerjewels that support your movement forward.

"Remember, the less baggage you carry while mastering the Alchemy of Change, the more Enerjewels you can accumulate. The more excess baggage you have, the more weight and influence your Ego can exert." The teacher began illustrating the points he'd just made with what appeared to be luxuriant clouds of chalk dust.

"Psssssst! Peter help! What's all these Enerjewels?"

"It's simple. Look at it this way. You've chosen to be a researcher, right? You are willing to learn, enjoy and keep moving on your path by continually changing, trading in your experience for each next step. There is lots of hidden energy in many forms to be discovered on your path—these are the Enerjewels. Sometimes the energy comes in the form of support, other times in the ability to be compassionate and so on... Whatever you require at that stage in your learning, the Enerjewel will enable you to achieve it. They are both a result and something that keeps you going in the greater cycle of change.

"To be able to discover Enerjewels you've got to learn from your experience and clear space within you to store them. The more you have, the more you empower yourself to create a conscious Life. This means there's less room for conditioning and Ego. If you let your Ego take over the research trip then it'll monopolize your company until it has complete control and then you'll end up going around and around in Existence."

"Okay," I whispered, "here's a quick summary: choose change, understand the path, trade Ego in for progress, gain the hidden treasure, live happily ever after,"

"Yes that's it. Now quiet. He's about to start again."

"Thanks Peter," I said under my breath.

Mr Baxter rubbed the excess chalk off his hands and launched into his next monologue.

"When you are in control, denial or resistance on your journey, then your progress can be stop-start. That is, until you release the Ego that is holding you back. When experiencing the greatest of polarities or extremes, you may feel like you are being dragged relentlessly through the situation kicking and screaming. Alternatively, at the other extreme, you become frustrated, thinking there is some universal conspiracy holding you back. These experiences are all just illusions of the mind. In all cases, extreme or not, what you are required to do is face your experience." He returned to the board writing F-A-C-E in extravagant capitals.

"F-A-C-E stands for Flexibility, Awareness, Commitment and Expect-the-unexpected. If you are always flexible and committed to your research, you will always be open to learning and to the opportunities of an unlimited creation stream, otherwise known as the 'Grand Flow' of 'going-with-the-flow' fame. The Grand Flow is the fuel of the Alchemy of Change. The more conscious going-with-the-flow you can achieve, the more change you will enable and the grander the flow will become.

"If you are aware, you will be able to gather both understanding and wisdom during each cycle of changement. If you always expect the unexpected, you will consolidate all of your changes and pass each Initiation. The Alchemy Of Change will then become natural as you welcome the opportunity to recycle your resistances over and over again."

Mr Baxter paused to consult his notes for his next diagram.

'Great, another break,' I thought as I was gasping for academic oxygen.

"Pssst Peter. Another emergency recap required. Just hear me out... So the fuel for our path forward is always there if we are prepared to F-A-C-E our experience. The more we face our experience and gain the Enerjewels, the more conscious we become. As we process the cycles of change we can go with the flow more and more until we co-create completely with the Grand Flow and can create anything, so long as it's loving, right?"

"Yep."

"But what's initiation?"

"Shhhhhh," hushed Peter, almost without moving his lips, and keeping his eyes forward.

"So to recap, here is the equation for the cycle of change," said Mr Baxter, cleaning the board and then proceeding to fill its length with the equation of change.

RESPONSE — REJOICEMENT — RELINQUISHMENT

"Remember," said Mr Baxter turning and scanning all the rows in the classroom with a clarifying gaze. "Just because you start the cycle doesn't mean you will complete it. If Ego is allowed to dominate this equation at any time, you will remain at the stage you have reached until you are able to change your mind and perception, overcoming the Ego obstacle in your path. Allow me to explain…

"If you encounter Ego in the Response phase, then you are likely to react. Reaction is set off by Ego. It can only perpetuate conflict and rebuild your resistance in a more complicated form. When you are in Response, you are allowing the flow of change.

"If you encounter Ego within Rejoicement, you may simply find it difficult to appreciate the experience you have created or be unwilling to believe that you can create anything more fulfilling than the experience you are within.

"Have you ever heard yourself say 'It doesn't get better than this'? Well, I hope not because in the Alchemy Of Change there is always, I repeat *always*, the potential for your level of awareness, fulfillment and wisdom to expand. The choice is yours."

He paused dramatically, lowering his glasses and

squinting into the rows of students, to punctuate the importance of his point.

"This however," he continued, maintaining his sternness, "could easily be overlooked if you allow your Ego to compare your present with your past and lock you into consequence, one of the products of Ego. So don't! Every single moment in this class is full of unlimited creation. Only the perception of Limitation stands between you and your dreams. The rate at which you bring your dreams into your experience is a function of how much Ego excess baggage you try to carry on your path. The more Ego you hold on to, the harder it will be. The less Ego you allow to influence you, the more direct and easier your path." He paused.

"Yes. Well we are at exactly half way through the material I wanted to cover today. Any questions?"

The room was silent. So silent I wondered if others could hear my thoughts. This was definitely re-learning learning. I was now convinced that if school had been as liberating as this, I would never have spent my time scattering my creativity through periods of rebellion. Mr Baxter interrupted my internal commentary.

"What a wise group I have today," observed Mr Baxter with a grin. "No questions at all... I will continue... "If you encounter Ego within the Relinquishment phase, then Ego will use your own fear of lack against you. If you believe that you can't continue to collect Enerjewels and your understanding of the Alchemy Of Change, Ego will start to build a comfort zone in order to convince you that there is no point in going beyond it. So what is to be done?"

Mr Baxter threw the question in our direction but quickly thought better of it. Unwilling to relinquish his verbal momentum, he started answering it himself.

"Listening to your Heart, not your head, will ensure that you feel your progress forward instead of losing touch with it through Ego interference. The more cycles of change you undergo, the greater your awareness of change will be and the greater will be your ability to harness the Grand Flow. All is available, but it is wisdom that allows the rate of availability to increase. The more wisdom, the more capability you will embrace and the more momentum you will gain.

"When you all become masters of this discipline, your Heart, creations and the Universe will synchronize as one. Hopefully this is an inspiration that will sustain you through the process." He paused to emphasize this potential achievement.

"Think of your first experiments within the Alchemy Of Change akin to building a house. With limited awareness you won't really have an overall vision of the materials you are using and what you actually want the house to look like. But with each passing cycle of change you will start to synchronize what you think with what you feel. As a result, what you think you are creating and what you want to create will unify. The more cycles of change you undergo, the clearer and more accurate the design of your house will be until you are able to build what you want and enjoy it... and then be happy to dismantle it in favor of the next installment of your continually expanding vision. Nothing will be too good, too true or too much. When you believe you have built all of your dreams, you will find new ones because you will truly understand that the flow is endless.

"If the Alchemy Of Change teaches you one thing, it's that there is always more flow when you are ready to F-A-C-E your experience. Through Transformation and Transmutation, you will harness more and more of the Grand Flow of creation and become the alchemists you seek.

"We'll now break for five minutes before the summary and today's practical."

"Close your mouth," said Peter.

I didn't realize I was gaping with astonishment at the lecture we'd just received.

"That's basic stuff. We're nowhere near advanced yet. There's four more classes before we get to that level."

"Just as well," I gulped. "I'm having enough trouble wrapping my head around this. I never knew there was so much in learning. It's a whole way of life. I'm using perception muscles I didn't know I had. My brain hurts!"

"Well you better start limbering up — Baxter's coming back. When he says five minutes, it's never a moment longer." Mr Baxter swept back into the class room exactly on time. "Please be seated. Hurry up, I'm not prepared to spend a moment of this passing age waiting for you lot to sit down. I have better things to do and be with my Enerjewels." His eyebrows raised almost to his hairline and the class settled into silence.

"So, to recap:

"Phase 1 — Response: Choosing to respond means keeping your Heart and mind open when it is easy to shut both through reaction. As you replace reaction with Response, you will build the ability to respond — responsibility. The more responsibility you can harness, the more you will be aware and able to create learning and create what you want. You may think you know what you want but going through the Alchemy Of Change will show you if you really do know or if you just think you know.

"Phase 2 — Rejoicement: Rejoicing allows you to expand your Heart and your awareness of your creation capability. When joy flows through you, you are at one with the Grand Flow rather than the flow that your mind tells you is available to you. Rejoicement is vital because it gives you the space to consolidate learning and to appreciate what you have created. After all, creation is a joy, not a struggle!

"Phase 3 — Relinquishment: This is the final phase in the Alchemy Of Change. It is the last stage of understanding and gives the opportunity to apply what you have learnt to create wisdom. During Relinquishment, always remember the Grand flow is endless — As one door closes another door opens; With a death comes a rebirth. All these phrases are designed to teach you one thing; there is no end, only flow. Ego will try and tell you that you've reached your learning limit and there is nothing more you can do. But resisting Relinquishment will trap you in an experience that is beyond its sell-by date and can only drain your Enerjewels and stop your progress."

The class was completely silent. Mr Baxter appeared to have driven his point home.

"So, before we relinquish this learning experience, what is the single word we can use to describe the Alchemy Of Change?"

"Recycling," came the reply from the third row.

"Precisely. The fourth R — Recycling," concluded Mr Baxter with a triumphant edge to his voice. "You didn't expect another R did you? But we are unlimited creators, practicing our art. So we appreciate the unexpected.

"No experience of any cycle of change is wasted. The more space you make within yourself, the more Ego you are recycling. The more resistance, fear and control you convert, the more Enerjewels you accumulate. Remember, nothing is destroyed nor created; all is a flow. In truth, the Enerjewels that you create are the product of the recycling of Ego.

You look surprised, class. Wonderful. What would the Alchemy of Change be without the surprises?"

Mr Baxter paused, almost hypnotizing the whole class with the peace in his eyes. He was fulfilled as he reached the end of this particular Alchemy of Change.

"One last point. If you are going to master the Alchemy of Change, you would do well to remember this. There are no failures, only learning. If you wish to listen to Ego, it will tell you that you fail regularly when your cycle of change doesn't work out the way you planned. But it's all an illusion. The only one who has failed is Ego because you are no longer limited by its perceptions and you are one step closer to understanding the great mystery of the Grand Flow."

Mr Baxter's wisdom echoed through the class and the bell rang.

"Please be back in ten minutes for your next installment of uncertainty. Class dismissed!"

Bubble, bubble, toil and trouble

I was in mind-shock. I'd never been to a lecture like it. What a great change to actually learn something that I could apply to everyday Life instead of learning how to fit in and to complicate and perpetuate Existence.

When we came back from our break the lecture room had transformed into a shrubbery of small chemistry sets. My heart sank.

"I thought this was a philosophy class," I whispered to Peter.

"It is," he replied, unphased.

"So why have we got Bunsen burners and distillation sets?"

"Because this is the practical... 'Expect the unexpected' — remember. It's easy. Just look in front of you. There are trays of compounds. This is the formula sheet. Mix A & B, bring to the boil, distil, add distilled product to compound C, and so on... Just follow the instructions."

"Thanks. Sorry to be a pain. I don't feel that confident about practicals."

"Who does? But of course, that's the whole point: F-A-C-E your experience. Besides, we've all got our blind spots. I'm happy to help."

I mixed A and B on a low heat and the combination released red and orange sparks, the mixture remaining a rich saffron. My attention wandered to the bench in front where all the other mini cauldrons were alive with a bright pink commotion.

"How come yours is bright pink?" I asked Peter, feeling sure I'd followed the steps exactly.

"Don't worry about it. That's how it is. Just carry on."

"But shouldn't I start again? Get fresh compounds?"

"No, no, carry on with what you've got. Just add it to C and so on. It'll all come right, you'll see," Peter replied without looking at the obvious color differences.

I carried on trying to rise above my sinking feeling. Bringing the mixture to the boil, it turned a bright pink and I was relieved. But then it changed again, becoming a bright aqua. I turned to look around the lab but everyone appeared to be at different stages of the formula sheet. Peter was already onto the last distillation.

I recorded the colors at each stage, hoping that somehow all my wrongs could change into rights. After forty-five minutes all the hissing, fizzing and foaming fluorescence had ceased. There were three vessels: one green, one deep blue and one aqua. Peter had finished twenty minutes previously but had spent a focused fifteen minutes writing notes. I sat on my stool, happy to relinquish my results and hoping the postmortem wouldn't be too protracted.

Seeing that everyone had completed their tests, Mr Baxter cleared his throat and began asking for questions and comments. I kept my head down hoping he wouldn't notice my sea of blue-green in amongst the shoreline of earthy tones that surrounded me.

"How can all the results be so varied?" asked Mr. Baxter, straight to the jugular.

"Because we are all individuals," answered the second row.

"Precisely. Any other reason? The student at the back... next to Peter please stand up and tell us how you would interpret your results?"

I stood up awkwardly and prepared to stammer a reply.

"Expect the unexpected," I began, surprising myself with my focus.

"Sorry, I can't quite hear you. Can you speak up?" I cleared my throat.

"Part of facing our experience is expecting the unexpected. I thought I would get the same answer as everyone else because I went through the same set of equations and processes. But that didn't happen. This particular Alchemy of Change is showing us that there aren't any right or wrong answers, just different ones, and it's up to us to work out what our answer means to us."

"Go on." Said Baxter, looking more intently over rather than through his glasses.

"Peter doesn't have the right answer with his reddish brown compounds but neither do I with my blues and greens. The different colors simply mean we are at a different stage in our own personal Alchemy Of Change; a different part of the cycle perceived through an individual perspective. The important element is we learn from our own colorful creations.

"I didn't think that my philosophy would be applied in a chemical way but now I can see that the whole point of our Alchemy of Change is that change is all around us — it's like we are part of one big chemical reaction. (Well, response is probably a more appropriate word). So why wouldn't change apply here? I must admit, I don't particularly enjoy practicals but just because I felt uneasy doesn't mean I couldn't learn. The room was silent. I felt strangely liberated from my insecurities I continued...

"The Enerjewel I reclaimed today came as a result of the belief that I can always learn irrespective of my knowledge or surroundings. I've dismantled some of the structures in my mentality that have held my ignorance. Now I have more fuel to learn and less to maintain my resistance to learning.

"The understanding I've processed today is that I have a tendency to let the external authority run my Life. I thought I had the wrong answer because I didn't fit in. I put 'following the herd' as more important than following my own heart and intuition.

"So in conclusion, the wisdom I've distilled today is *Create from the Heart, not the herd*. Listen to the inner authority of the Heart and don't live in the shadow of others' judgments; wisdom doesn't come from getting the right or even wrong answers, it comes from choosing to apply what you learn." I sat down.

Baxter paused. Was that a ripple of teacher's pride I saw dissolve into his dry persona?

"Thank you. A concentrated and illuminating discourse." He paused a second time as if suspended in the moment.

"Your words were pure gold dust," whispered Peter. "You've definitely got a future in alchemy, particularly if you can render Baxter speechless!"

Baxter closed his textbook and put his glasses in his breast pocket. "And so," he began, "here endeth the lesson. Next class Thursday at four sharp and, as always, expect the unexpected. Class dismissed."

Fear's gold

I thought I'd be relieved to get out of the chemistry class but instead there was no great impetus to rush anywhere.

"What are you doing for lunch?" I asked Peter.

"Nothing."

"Do you want to snack under the oak tree and answer a few more questions about the Alchemy Of Change?" I suggested.

"Sure, why not. But maybe all you require is the time to let it sink in. You seem to be getting the hang of it."

"Well, I am and I'm not. I'm definitely hanging, just not quite sure what's on the other end! It's an interesting sensation.

Should I free fall from where I'm hanging or should I climb back to what I think is familiar?"

"Well, you're definitely way past the edge, so just go into free fall. Nothing is going to happen to you that you can't learn from or understand."

We sat on a rich carpet of grass, shaded from the hottest part of the day by the hospitable oak. Lunch boxes full with fresh sandwiches never seemed to finish, no matter how much we ate.

"The part of the Alchemy Of Change that intrigues me is the recycling bit. Why bother to recycle if the Universe has an unending flow? Wouldn't it be simpler to throw out what isn't working and concentrate on what is?"

"Well, first of all, the flow is endless because nothing is destroyed. You can't throw yourself away; it's not possible because the Alchemy Of Change is 100% efficient. The unity is always maintained, even if you aren't aware of it fully. Cutting out bits of yourself that you don't understand makes your path very difficult. All you'll achieve is scattering or isolating those parts of yourself in Existence, controlled by Ego, and that will make your return to RealLife a lot harder. If you try to throw a part of yourself away at some point you will have to go back and get it some time later to reunite the whole.

"Remember we're researchers. There are no bits of our research that aren't helpful, even the bits full of Ego. They are all research. So there's no reason to throw away bits that aren't working. They've been working before but now you've changed your perspective, you'd like them to work differently. Love, compassion and understanding will bring about this change. So there is nothing wrong with you or any part of your research."

"So Peter, it's more a question of research in different areas and in different ways."

"Yes. You've researched what it's like to be in the middle

of Ego, now you're researching what it's like to look from Life into Ego and then Life into RealLife and so on and so forth. The nature of your research was a lot more limited when you were in Existence... and understandably. That was what you were researching — how to be limited. Now you've got a lot of new directions and facets of research available. That's why you can only coordinate all these directions through your Heart. If you tried to do it through your mind, you'd explode."

"A messy business."

"Quite!" laughed Peter.

"I'm a pictures type of person. If you could now put me in terms of a diagram, like the emotional, physical and mental circles of before, then how would you do it?"

"Okay... Think of yourself as a cake divided into segments. The size of each slice can change according to the choices that you make. Each slice represents an aspect of yourself. Now that you are on your journey of discovery, you are choosing to understand all the aspects of yourself. Let's call segment 1 and 2 Fear and Denial respectively. When you started your research in Limitation these slices took up nearly all the area of the cake."

"But what about now?" I interrupted feeling an upsurge of justification. "That's not how I want to harness my energy now."

"Exactly. Don't worry, I'm not judging you into a corner, I'm in your corner. I'm agreeing with you! The whole point of being here is to learn, right?"

"Yep."

"So in your process of self discovery you want to find all the slices in the cake. You also want to change the size of the Fear and Denial portions. When you were in Limitation it was fine to divide yourself predominantly within this area. But you aren't there any more. When you chose to change, your cake began to divide itself up very differently. You discovered slice

3: Choice. Ever since this you've been committed to finding alternatives and 3 has been increasing in size and 1 and 2 have been getting smaller. Most recently you discovered 4 which is Truth and so the cake reapportioned itself yet again. And so it goes on."

"So the more I change, the more slices of the whole I will find?"

"Absolutely."

"So when do I get to have my cake and eat it?" I joked.

"Well it's more to know your cake and fully appreciate it for its wholeness. When you have unity you don't need to consume it to be it. You become it. The cake is, after all, only an analogy for the state of unity you can achieve. You are currently on that journey of reunification with the Grand Flow. With each Alchemy of Change you undergo, there will come a point where you understand all the segments of yourself, and when 1 and 2 finally disappear you will have mastered your Alchemy of Change—you will have your cake and be it!"

"So fundamentally, the more aware you become, the more you can understand each individual segment of yourself and thus the whole?"

"Yes. And the more practice you get, the smoother the phases of change will become. The more aware you become in general, the less resistance you have and the more Enerjewels available to create your Life wisely and smoothly."

"Simple, really!" I joked, screwing up my face at the complexity of the task.

"You never said a truer word. It's an endless flow of change. All you are required to do is go through the small changes and then the Initiations. You asked me about that before, remember?"

"Yes. I didn't quite get what Baxter was talking about with Initiation."

"Initiation is a complete shift in perception and awareness.

All the smaller Alchemies Of Change have added up to build enough momentum to move into the next higher level of awareness. It's like in chemistry, we study certain reactions individually then we put them all together and the combined energy creates a completely new state or compound."

"So it's a bit like the difference between the two sessions today."

"What do you mean?" Peter was puzzled.

"Well, when I went into what I *thought* was a philosophy, I was thinking one way and didn't know even if that was what I should be doing. Then after adapting to relearning, I ended up facing the challenge of applying philosophy to a chemistry experiment. I could have easily overlooked or resisted the connection between them."

"Yes. Your initiation required a huge amount of flexibility. You changed your mind and then applied that totally new way of thinking in the flow. You didn't stop the momentum by dissecting your situation, you trusted and moved beyond your existing belief barriers."

"How do you know that for sure?" I insisted.

"It's not a matter of knowing, it's a matter of feeling — recognizing the nature of your experience. Take Baxter's question; you could have fudged it or refused to answer it but you didn't. You got on a roll of how you felt. You didn't say what your fearful convention and logic wanted, nor did you give up or throw your compounds away. You accepted your Inner Authority, not your Ego. You let go of knowing and trusted the unknown and your intuitive interpretations. You accommodated the unexpected instead of running away from it."

"I suppose you're right, when you put it like that."

"Well, now you've done it you can look back and understand it fully. It's very important to realize you don't need to know or even understand that you are in the state of Initiation, all you are required to do is demonstrate your commitment. You passed the test by recycling your ignorance, fear and self doubt. An instantaneous shift in belief happened; a mini miracle—you changed your mind,"

"Sounds wonderful," I said, relaxing completely into the grass.

"It is."

"So it's floating on a sea of wisdom from now on?" I pretended to float on an imaginary inflatable.

"Not quite. You can't float around forever with only one Initiation to your credit! But it's a great start. What you'll be discovering soon is the acceptance and belief in yourself to take it further, to progress. The Alchemy Of Change is one non-stop change train. It can also be a roller coaster depending on how balanced you are. Non-stop change means non-stop expansion and that's the progress that you want. The more ready you are to recycle your fear, the more easily you can get through the peaks and troughs. Then your sea of wisdom will becalm. No more tidal waves or tropical cyclones; the sea of wisdom becomes and remains as flat as a mill pond!"

"So, what's it like out the other side, the other side of Initiation, that is?"

"Well, the same… but different. The Transformations and Transmutations are still there, but first you'll have a period of assimilation, a bit like now. Call it a fuel stop. There is always more choice after Initiation. There is also a new distribution of your resources."

"So how's my pie chart looking now?" I enquired optimistically.

"Not too flabby! After your Initiation, I think you can safely say Ego is occupying a much smaller percentage of you now. Anyway, who care's about quantities?" As Baxter always says, it's qualities that count! The most important result is that you're leaving fear behind. There's no going back. But that's fine because you don't want to go back to Existence. Or do you?"

"No, no. I've done my linear time there! I don't want to spend my Enerjewels subsidizing fear. I'm much better off cashing them in during Initiation and moving to the next level. So, how do you differentiate between the big shifts and the small shifts within the Alchemy Of Change?"

"I call the small changes within a cycle Transformations. When Initiation is completed then the total change is Transmutation—that's the complete shift from one frequency of energy and awareness to the next. We can waver during Transformations, go back and forth if you like, but not with Transmutations. Once you've Initiated out of a certain way of experiencing, you can't go back, no matter how hard you try."

What goes around, comes around

Peter fell silent and stared across the lawn towards the library. He turned to face me again as if anticipating my last question.

"I've got one last question. What happens when we both graduate from being apprentices to being Masters of Alchemical Change?"

Peter was silent for a moment considering his reply. "We will be able to adapt to the Grand Flow by creating and recycling simultaneously. We'll be unending just like a giant sphere, connected in all directions to our experience."

"Sounds busy, Peter."

"Perhaps, but gaining this ability is only as complicated as our minds would like to make it. At the higher levels of awareness, it isn't about your doingness, or effort, it's more to do with your ability to remain in the center of your Heart and your experiences. Everything goes on around you and through you; you are within it, but you aren't trying to control it logically with your mind.

"Hard to contemplate at this stage because we still have so much of our energy tied up in mental control. We've been conditioned by Ego to control every creative opportunity through our minds, not embrace them through our hearts. So that's why re-learning is so important. Before, we learnt via Ego so we could research Limitation. Now we're learning through Heart so we can embrace expansion and the unlimited. With more trust, there is less desire to control — there is no reason to control something we no longer fear."

"So can we just forget about our Ego at the higher frequencies? Does it fall out of the equation of change completely?"

"No, but the way we relate to it changes and its relationship with us becomes more subtle, though still potentially highly imbalancing."

"But surely that's a contradiction. The less we allow Ego to influence us, the less impact it can have on us, right?"

"The more progress we make, the higher and more potent the bands of energy and consciousness we reach. Yes, at these levels of awareness we are less likely to let our Ego run our Life, but Ego compensates for that by becoming more subtle and more sneaky. The higher the band of energy, the more empowered we are to create what we want. But Ego can still knock us out of our center and blow our experience of minor fear and resistance out of all proportion. All it takes is one reaction."

"Like a spark near a gas leak?"

"Exactly. The Ego waits for its opportunity and when the conditions are right it tries to get you to spark. Then what is a minor friction, which wouldn't normally bother you, turns into a major upset."

"What happens next?"

"Ego controls your energy and you collapse temporarily into Existence. When this happens it takes a lot of centeredness and self discipline to shift back into Life. It can be overcome but it's a valuable reminder of just how powerful Ego can be. That's why there are so many small Transformations. As you go through these, it is less likely that Ego will be hidden in the many layers of yourself waiting to ambush you. Also, by the point of Initiation you will have had a lot of practice at dealing with Ego so change will be much more manageable.

"You'll always meet a piece of your Ego during each Initiation, but your intention is that you will be able to walk through your Ego and out the other side rather than get caught up in protracted negotiations, arguments or the seeking of approval."

"So Peter, from now on, Ego will be more subtle, but that doesn't mean any less effective?"

"Exactly. Ego is just as destructive and attractive as it has always been, ready to be the short cut of your dreams, which actually turns out to be the fast track to Limitation."

"So if I were Ego, surely I'd sit around watching and waiting until my host got to Initiation and then try and stop them."

"Well, yes, that's the logical approach, but fortunately Initiation isn't logical!" laughed Peter. "That's why, if we Expect the unexpected, we will always be able to change irrespective of the circumstances. Ego can't compete against the chaos of the cosmos because it functions through the order of Limitation. So Ego will bluff and double bluff, but once we've chosen Initiation, the exact moment remains a mystery. Ego gets conned into thinking it's important while what is really significant happens right under its nose, so to speak."

"Some trick."

"Well Ego's the best illusion artist in the world, so it's always got to be good to keep it occupied."

"So if I can change the subject a little... if Ego runs Limitation, what or who runs RealLife?"

"Your Higher Self, of course."

"So where is my Higher Self exactly?"

"Higher Self dwells in RealLife. It can come into Life and send messages to Existence but they don't register there. We can only utilize it's support in Life and RealLife. Ego tries to drown any Higher Self messages that reach Existence, but if we manage to hear them we will wake up and smell the 'expansion' and it won't be long before we have at least sampled what Life has to offer."

"So your Higher Self can rescue you?" I teased.

"No, absolutely not. No rescue missions allowed, only invitations. Everything is still a choice. There are plenty who hear their Higher Self and make an excursion out of Limitation, only to return when they realize the magnitude of the change that's required to stay in the land of the Living. There's nothing wrong with their decision because everything is a choice. The Higher Self will still be of service to the person but that doesn't mean they are going to do anything about the guidance. Learning is a choice as well. Not everyone chooses to be a conscious Researcher. You know that from your time in Heaven Can Wait."

"The Existors, you mean?"

"Yes. They are happy with learning about Existing and Limitation. Whereas you, on the other hand, have chosen to discover choice and convert that into being a conscious Researcher. The more you choose to change, the more you can communicate with your Higher Self. Mystery turns into magic and as we know from philosophy and chemistry it is the matter of Mastery. Existing in Limitation is just one big cosmic joke that only becomes funny when you've left Existence!"

"So if I want more RealLife, I choose to communicate more with my Higher Self?"

"Well yes, that's part of it. But it's also a state of endless feeling when you have no fear, only love and the allowance of the Grand flow."

"Well Peter, this has been one hell — sorry, one *heaven* of a working lunch. I feel saturated with learning!"

"Indeed. Time to stop. I need to go to the library. Do you want to come to avoid going soggy?"

"No, I'll risk it. I'm so relaxed, I really don't want to move."

"Okay. Far be it from me to disturb the Sleep Researcher. You must have been awake now all of three hours so you'll be ready for another power nap."

"I'm relaxed," I protested, "not sleepy. There's a subtle difference you know! But before you go, Peter, tell me how come you know so much? I'll rephrase that. You feel so deeply about your subject, it's almost as if you should be teaching. Either that or you're the most enthusiastic student I've ever met. Why don't you take Baxter's place next class?"

"What are you, the Sleeping Prophet now?"

"What do you mean?" I was taken aback.

"Trust your intuition."

"You mean you're really a teacher?!"

"Yes. From next Monday I'm on class practice, re-learning like you!"

"You've lost me again."

"Remember: Expect the unexpected! Don't assume that in a class of students there is only one teacher. We're both re-learning learning. I'm re-learning what it's like to be a student in the classroom. That's why I was sitting next to you. You're new and required a little extra tutoring."

"So this is a setup, be it a very helpful one."

"Call it a learn up; getting you in tune with the way of learning you've forgotten. The best teachers are always the ones who never forget to learn. Sleep well!"

"I'm not sleeping, just surrendering!" I called after Peter as he headed in the direction of the library. 'I'm surrendering to the possibility that I'll never work this out,' I said to myself, propping my back against the tree and closing my eyes.

Out the other side

Of course Peter was right. The gentle summer breeze, the shade of the mature oak and six sandwiches made the perfect recipe for a snooze. On the sounds of summer, I drifted high into the trees, supported by the lush countryside greens. My transition was easier this time and when I opened my eyes I was almost expecting to see Michael. Well, almost.

"Having a nice time sleeping your way to wisdom?" Michael joked as he pressed an old penny into my hand and draped a coat around my shoulders.

"Well, the Alchemy Of Change has taught me that I can learn from each moment of my experience, so why not in my sleep?"

"Why not, indeed," said Michael, smiling at my precocious reply.

"Is it evening, already?" I could smell chestnuts roasting and hear cries of enjoyment and fairground music. "Are we at a fairground, Michael?"

"Yes. Do you like amusements?"

"Well, I used to. Seems an age since I went on a ghost train or the big dipper."

"Shall we have a go?" Michael gestured like a showman presenting an act.

"Why not."

I walked towards the sounds of Madi Gras jazz and cheering crowds but there were so many people and so many stalls that I felt like I was going around in circles. Michael fell behind, held up by a sudden crowd of candy floss consumers. The more I waited for him, the further behind he seemed to be. I began to feel disorientated as I passed a stall for the second time when I was sure I had taken a new direction. There was an old fashioned mirror-and-magic show at the end of the row and I decided to go in. I reached into my pocket and gave the attendant my penny.

She took it and I filed into the display, the last in a long stream of people.

The first room was pitch dark apart from a few strategically placed floor lights. I followed the lights and entered another room which appeared to be the promised Hall Of Mirrors. The light remained dim but I caught glimpses of the people ahead, first a face like a blow fish then a dwarf wearing oversized clothes and glasses that took over their whole face. Then I saw my own emaciated reflection only to bloat to the size of a professional wrestler with my next step. Laughter echoed around the exhibit but I couldn't laugh; I found the whole place bizarre, even unnerving.

I moved to what appeared to be the exit to the magic show mini theatre but I found still more mirrors. I was becoming thirsty and frustrated. I saw another door reflected in the first mirror but it also lead back into the same room.

I was now uneasy and agitated. I started to blame my environment for my frustrations. This was meant to be funny, not frightening. I was just about to bang on the walls for assistance when a door opened inwardly and the magician who was obviously waiting for the last member of his audience, offered me his hand. I felt a complete idiot, holding up the show and getting so upset, all over a few mirrors.

The magic show helped me get my experiences back into perspective. A combination of magic and humor dispelled my grey anxiety. I was surprised and delighted to see Michael standing at the exit as the curtain fell.

"So how was it?" he asked, obviously eager to hear my response.

"To be honest, it was quite frightening at first. I got caught up in all the confusion and distortions of the mirror room. My fear seemed to distort and intensify as I tried to find a way out. I couldn't get out until the magician opened the door. What on Earth is all that supposed to mean? I found it really disturbing."

"If I'd told you before you went there, you wouldn't have been able to experience it."

"You knew about this?" I felt a twinge of betrayal. "You knew I would go through that and you didn't do anything to stop me? A big help you are! I thought you were supposed to be guiding me."

"Yes, that's correct; it is my service. But guiding you doesn't mean doing your path for you. You are still required to realize your own path. No one can do that for you."

"So what's the difference between walking the path and making self loving choices? Did I make the wrong choice going in there? Did I interpret my feelings wrongly? Could I have had a better experience?"

"No, you had the experience that was part of your current flow of learning. You had the one you planned for yourself. You had the experience of coming out the other side of your Initiation and consolidating into your new environment, the new level of awareness and energy. You achieved this despite your Ego's attempts to stop you. You met the Magician, which means you managed to navigate through a whole cycle of the Alchemy Of Change. So congratulations are in order."

"So why all the disruption? Why was it so hard to get to the Magician? Surely if I have achieved the Initiation, there's a little break? A pay-off and celebration for my achievement?"

"Yes, this is it now. It's just that you're still in the emotional reactions and attachments of your recent past. Give it a few minutes and you'll have caught up with yourself."

I shrugged my shoulders and walked in the direction of the chestnut seller. I bought two packets. I was just about to walk back to Michael when I turned around and bumped into him.

"Some light refreshment?" he smiled peacefully.

"Yes. Do you want some? Here, I bought you a packet."

"Thank you. Are they part of your celebration?" asked Michael hopefully.

"Yes, alright, alright you win."

"Really, I thought it was you doing the winning and I was just observing your achievement."

"Well whatever it is I'm prepared to take a few steps in a positive direction," I replied, relinquishing some of my grumpiness.

"Wonderful. Sometimes the first steps in the new awareness are like that—a sort of settling in; a bit of a bumpy ride, but not always. Often your Ego tries to discourage you, slow your acceleration as you get into the new energy level. Ego sets off little panic or exaggeration incendiaries to try and slow you down. But if you don't let these little interludes blow you off course, they are all over pretty quickly."

"So all I was doing was getting acclimatized to a new cycle of learning?"

"Yes, and you succeeded because you didn't try and destroy your environment or the message within it. You went through your experience and you came out the other side."

"Well, can I arrange a less bumpy ride next time? Surely there is an easier way. If I am responsible for all my choices, I can choose something easier right?"

"Yes and no."

"Meaning *yes* there is and I didn't create it, or *no* because in my case there isn't?"

"Currently, you have chosen to process your research and your Initiations the accelerated way."

"But I decided that before I knew how it was going to be in the practical, right?"

"Sort of. Other parts of you—the ones that are in RealLife—chose the intense route with your consent."

"Why?"

"With the Alchemy Of Change, choice is indeed the vehicle, but you can drive that vehicle at various speeds. Because you chose acceleration, or fast track, the cycles of change can appear more intense. It has it's advantages, it's just not everyone's cup of tea. Others choose a less speedy rate of realization. As always, it's all choice."

"So it's like the tortoise and the hare?"

"Well not really. There is no competition, no 'them and us', just different. Some individuals choose fast track, others a more leisurely pace. All get to the same destination. It's simply a case of a different way of experiencing the path."

"So if I understand rightly, when I first get through an Initiation, there's a period of adjustment out the other side?"

"Yes."

"During which I am to remain calm and try and keep my balance rather than reacting and dragging Ego back into my experience equation."

"Exactly."

"If I want to accelerate my Alchemy Of Change then I am required to go fast track… which means that from time to time my experience of my changes could get really intense, weird or appear to be at the very edge of my personal acceptability rating!"

"Yes."

"What if I want to renegotiate my rate of processing?"

"This is, of course, a choice. You may."

"But you already know that I won't, right?"

"Put it this way: once you have acclimatized to your path of acceleration you are unlikely to want to change it. This is because the first change is always the most difficult and, well… you're through that now."

"But Michael, you can only say that because I've completed it."

"You're learning! I wouldn't have been able to tell you before this because…"

I interrupted. "Because then I would find a way not to go through it?"

"Precisely. You would simply make energetic excuses and give Ego way too much of your valuable Enerjewels, making it a lot harder to move forward."

"So, if you don't mind, now can I take a break?"

"Yes, of course. Another sleep?"

"Well, when I go to sleep I'm always traveling somewhere. So I don't really want a fake sleep, I want a genuine one with lots of rest. And while I'm reviewing my choices, can I also have a learning environment that is more 'normal'?"

"You'll always find yourself in an appropriate learning environment, but I'll see how I can help with the rest. How about quality sleep with a little travel rolled in?"

"Is that what my Alchemy Of Change job description says? 'Sleep while maintaining agreed intensity'?"

"Something like that," replied Michael, his words begining to echo while his form started to fade at the edges.

Research in the field

"Can I open my eyes now?" I asked impatiently.

"Yes, of course you can," replied Michael.

"Where are we?"

"In a more everyday environment. You wanted more everyday, didn't you?"

"Yes, I did."

"Less bends, just a straight road ahead. So there you are."

A beautiful landscape stretched out before me, unfamiliar in itself but full of glimpses of places I used to know or had traveled through while researching previous assignments. The view that now stretched out before me was a breathtaking flourish of green. The road cut through a verdant fluorescence of wedding cake paddy fields bordered by emerald pastures with grazing cattle and bottle green trees ablaze with fiery blossom.

"Thank you... I think. This is truly beautiful. Does everything seem more beautiful at this level of energy, at this rate of acceleration?"

"When we spoke of intensity, it didn't mean the experience is negative. It can also be that your experience is intensely beautiful like this. It simply depends on your frame of mind."

Squinting hard, I could see what appeared to be a group of people in the distance.

"Who are those people up ahead?"

"They are your companions."

"But how can they accompany me if they are nowhere near me?"

"Distance is relative. Remember, I did say that as your Alchemy Of Change increases, Limitation may be seen to curve at certain points. Anyway, it's time to unleash you into the field for some intensive training."

"I don't think I like the sound of that."

"Don't think then; least of all presume, analyze or assume."

"Okay, okay. That's enough subtle and not-so-subtle hints. New band of energy; I create my reality; expect the unexpected and learn from it. It's like a surreal life coaching seminar. Face the fear and recycle it!"

"Welcome to your task," announced Michael with a ceremonious air, turning to greet the landscape.

I took this as encouragement and began striding ahead to catch up with the other participants. But the faster I walked the further away they appeared to be. Breaking out into a sweat was all the indication I needed to give up my chase, deciding instead to relax my vision into the scenery and a leisurely pace. As I walked in silence I could still feel someone walking behind me.

"Giving me the silent treatment now are you, Michael? Is this to help me merge with the group?"

But there was no reply. I glanced over my shoulder expecting to see Michael but all that greeted me was space. Still, the feeling persisted. I tried taking the space by surprise, but when I looked there was never anything there. I was alone and yet in the company of the indefinable.

"Okay Michael, I won't take it personally. You probably had someone else to guide so you've left me to my exploration."

"Who said you need a form to be your guide?" said a voice over my left shoulder.

"Who, indeed?" I asked myself as I turned around to be greeted by no one. "So you're also a master of disappearing acts then Michael?"

"Who said this was Michael?" came a faint reply that evaporated as soon as it reached my ears.

I searched for another question to ask to keep this intriguing conversation alive but there were no words and no other answers.

It appeared that I was now alone. In silence my journey wound smoothly through the valley, sloping slightly in my favor. I now had company in the form of a small stream bubbling parallel to the road. In the distance I could see a T-junction and a bridge. The leading individual cut across the bridge and turned left; those who followed turned right. My pace quickened as the first signpost I'd seen since we started our journey came into view. Much to my surprise and frustration, accelerating yielded the same rate of progress.

'More haste, less speed' I thought. Or was it that the air was thicker here than over there?

I breathed a sigh of relief as I reached the T-junction. I had an odd feeling of achievement but this soon dissolved into the need to decipher the road sign.

But the promise of information was disappointing. The weather-beaten slab of metal paled into insignificance in comparison to the majestic hills that rose up behind and to the right. It was as if one day a mythological giant, on a whim, had concertinaed the land into tightly packed curves leaving his mark as he passed through the wilderness.

"Gives a whole new meaning to landscaping" I murmured to the hot sun over head. But there was no sign of the giant now, just conifers huddling together on the exposed peaks and contours accompanied by the road clinging tightly around the bends as it climbed high into the distance.

I pulled my focus back and studied the sign. It read: 'Center Point Pass, right' and 'Headington, left.' Neither had any indication of distance. As the group had divided at this point I wondered which way was the right one to follow. At this rate I was going to be left behind completely. Feeling unsettled and devoid of inspiration, I decided to assess my options.

Turning right appeared to be an uphill climb all the way. I didn't have a car and walking up what appeared to be a small mountain would take forever. I couldn't imagine any way I would be able to rejoin the majority of the group on this terrain. I was just about to turn left when one of the group members to the right of me shouted down, "It's beautiful up here, you can see for miles. What are you waiting for?" The words echoed through the landscape and through my head.

I carried on my inner discussion, even though my co-participant had long disappeared from view. 'My first choice would be the hills, but I need to be practical.' I could feel my poor stamina levels weighing me down.

"No you're not," said a voice next to me. "You're being narrow minded, cube spirited. You're Existing. Haven't you had enough of that yet? What do you think this is, the physical world?"

I was taken aback. The voice was coming from a tree which shrugged its branches to drive its point home.

"No, it definitely isn't the physical world with a tree talking to me," I acknowledged wryly.

"So why are you thinking as if you were still in Limited Land?" the tree continued. "Just because it looks difficult in your mind doesn't mean it's difficult in your Heart.

Remember, your head thinks your Ego is the only source of help; your Heart knows there's a whole world of opportunity out there. You've got all the surroundings, including us. The nearest trees rustled their leaves in support. You want all the help you can get, right? Moreover, where's your Ego now?"

A flash of inspiration shone a golden beam into my rational gloom. "Ego has turned left, I suppose," I said without thinking, gesturing over the bridge.

"Now that wasn't so hard, was it? Remember, this is a Heart workout, not a brain teaser," the tree chuckled its foliage. "You're going to surprise yourself with just how easy this journey really is, once you truly meld with it."

A sudden breeze moved through the tree and across my face from left to right. I took the hint, followed the breeze and turned right. Looking at the steep incline, I decided to pace myself. I began to walk with an upsurge of self enquiry for company. My first question was why, after all the change I had already been through, had I still reverted to logic, seeking refuge in conditioning rather than trusting my intuition? I knew the answer but I was hoping to hear a different one. No whispering voices came to the rescue. Reluctantly I answered my own question. Logic was comfortable and habitual. I was still able to respond more quickly with my conditioning than my Heart.

My lungs were burning now, dry from the steep incline and the heat of the day. I decided to stop. If I carried on I would be by-passing my Heart, forcing myself to continue instead of choosing to.

It was time to halt my joy drain. I sat at the side of the road in the shade of a tree on fire with orange red blossom and inundated with buzzing bees.

"I'm getting left behind," I said aloud, beginning to slide into submission.

"Sorry, can't help those who are weighed down with resistance. As you can see, I've got productive responsibilities to attend to: no blossom — no bees; no bees — no berries." I looked around myself to see where the voice was coming from. I realized it was another tree.

"So what are you?"

"I'm a flaming tree."

"I can see that. There's no need to be rude!"

"Well there's no need to get offended. That's my name: Flaming Tree. As in 'tree on fire'... in my case, with blossom."

"Oh sorry, I get it, *flaming tree*... That's quite funny," I said, beginning to laugh. "In fact that's very funny." I dissolved into a fit of the giggles. "Are you the local stand up comic?"

"I could be easily but as you can see, I'm buzzy at the moment."

"Buzziness. That's a good one." I was now crying with laughter in the middle of nowhere, talking to yet another tree.

"Well you just carry on laughing your head off, it's the best therapy and the best infection you'll ever catch. Laughter is the lubricant of the Heart. If you ever want to kick start your Heart, just laugh... Well you better be on your way, get back up to speed. You don't want to be left behind, now do you?"

"No," I said jumping up with renewed energy after my laughter lube. "Thanks for the laughs. That really helped my internal valves. I'm firing on all cylinders now."

"You are most welcome. Now buzz off, I've got berries to grow!"

Heartfelt re-education

I felt like I was walking on air. My effort was finally synchronizing with my progress. I'd returned to going with the flow and was enjoying accelerated wellbeing. This was fitness I could handle. Willing steps had replaced my tired plod. It felt like I was beginning to fit in with the weird of the 'normal' I had co-created with Michael. I decided not to bother asking for 'normal' again because even if everything looked normal it was only a molecule deep before everything became weird again.

As I walked I kept thinking I saw faces or forms in the countryside. Mr Baxter's face flashed into my mind's eye. I wondered if he was going to materialize in front of me for yet another class of speed re-learning. But I had to be content with cumulus formations as they drifted effortlessly in the deep blue sky. 'Well, Mr Baxter,' I thought. 'As you aren't making an appearance today, I'll take my own class.'

I began lecturing the sky, writing equations on passing clouds. Here are the most recently researched equations of experience.

One: Fear + Ego + Mind = Limitation.

Two: Heart + Trust = Life.

Three: Heart + Trust + Higher Self = RealLife.

'Currently there are parts of me in all these worlds but I am flowing towards a time when I can concentrate my Enerjewels in RealLife. Homework, for now: finding my Higher Self.'

I quickened my pace, but not because I was eager to start my homework. My attention moved back to my desire to catch up with the main group. I hadn't seen any of the other participants since the group had shouted down to me at the T-junction. So as I rounded the next bend, I was astonished to glimpse what I assumed was everyone else getting into a group of cars and driving away.

"Wait for me!" I heard myself shout, but they continued to accelerate away as if I wasn't there.

Feeling rejected and disgruntled I continued walking, the weight of isolation bearing down on me.

"I suppose I'll have to walk the rest of the way," I muttered sulkily.

"Not unless you want to," came a reply, delivered in the beating wings of a passing bird.

"More calls of nature?" I joked weakly.

"Yes, actually. This is Nature calling. You're becoming more sensitive to my messengers. Congratulations. You can talk to a tree if you prefer."

"No," I said apologetically, my humor appearing completely out of place. "I was just sloshing through a few puddles of self pity. I'm disappointed that the others didn't wait for me. I just don't understand. I always seem to be the last one," I observed despondently.

"Well, perhaps you are the first of the many, not the last of the few," came an uplifting perspective.

I stopped walking. "I hadn't thought of it like that. Those in the leading group might not be leading at all. Actually, they are behind me and we are all traveling in a loop. I was just about to lap them." I started walking with renewed enthusiasm, having established an apparent competitive edge.

"Not exactly," said Nature. "Forget about competing with the others. Just devote your time to self enquiry, understanding yourself better. If you want to speed up, this will be the quickest way you will learn about your Heart. You want to be state-of-the-Heart, don't you?"

"Nice play on words. Yes I do. You're right, this isn't a race and we are all going at our own pace. I've got enough to understand without trying to compare myself with the group."

"Quite. That's expanding your vision rather than seeing what is on the surface. There are no conclusions here, only continuations; flows," Nature reassured me.

"I know... I mean, I *feel* what you are saying and it's registering in my Heart," I replied.

"Wonderful. Then you can appreciate that rewiring your Heart is a two way process. You nourish it with choice; it nourishes you by distributing this choice throughout your being and your experience. There is no cosmic wisdom that states that if others have, then you must do without. Remember, you are rewarding yourself irrespective of whether you are in front or behind. The unlimited flow is exactly that—unlimited. What you put in, you will experience as a result. Focus on what you want to create instead of slowing yourself down by wishing for the creations of another. There is plenty to go around; an unlimited abundance, to be more accurate."

"So, I can have a car too?" I said with a cheeky grin.

"Are you asking me or telling me?" enquired Nature.

"Both," I said, but I felt uneasy the moment the word came out of my mouth.

"In creation it is more helpful to focus on what you want rather than hedging your bets," replied Nature.

"Ha ha…Well, you'd know all about hedges," I said, laughing at the weak pun.

"Indeed," said Nature with a smiling tone.

"All right, I'm telling you: I would like a car," I committed reluctantly, feeling as if I was lazy or admitting weakness by not wanting to walk any further.

"Difficult to be honest about what you want?" observed Nature.

"Yes," I said, embarrassed at my unwillingness.

"It's okay to change." Nature paused. "No one said walking is better than driving. There is no one waiting to criticize your choice you know. Just make it from your Heart, forget about the others. Clarity reflects clarity—Cosmic Truth Number One! So what are you creating?"

"I am creating a car," I said, feeling better about wanting to drive. "So what's the next Truth?" I asked cheekily.

"Ask and ye shall receive. Look behind you," said Nature in a matter of fact way.

I turned around and there in the lay-by I had just passed was a red Mini with the number 8 painted on the roof.

"This will take you anywhere you want to go."

My first 100% Heart creation was right before me.

"Thank you, thank you," I stuttered in amazement and joy. "Thank you."

"It's our pleasure. But don't just thank us, thank yourself; it's your nature too! Amazing what you can create with some cooperation. Will fly now." Nature's voice began to fade into the exposed rocks and gatherings of trees.

"One last question before you go. What's the 8 for?" I said quickly, hoping Nature hadn't left.

"It's to remind you that what goes around comes around. Giving and receiving is one big infinity, whether its giving to yourself, receiving, helping another or a simultaneous combination of all."

"Thanks, Nature. And by the way, I won't worry about you leaving again. I understand now that you are all around."

"Yes. Anytime, any place, anywhere you want to be environmentally friendly, just call Nature. Remember, home is where the Heart is. You can never be helpless or without company if you remember that."

My logical mind was telling me that the car was a reward for being right or good. My Heart was telling me it was a reflection of my ability to believe that I could create what I wanted and that the Universe was a supportive place.

Quietening my mind, I hurried towards the Mini, the engine started without any hesitation. This was mini magic. It was responsive, courageous when it came to the steep inclines, and nimble around the corners. It was a pure joy to drive. So why, after my initial high had dissipated, was I feeling uneasy?

The feeling grew until I started worrying about hidden obstacles and oncoming traffic on the narrow road. 'The bad always comes with the good' echoed through my mind. 'What if you've failed the test and you should have continued walking?' came another voice. My head began to fill with all the possible problems that could arise. I pulled off the road for a moment and stopped the engine.

What was going on? What was I thinking? Did I think worry would make what I'd created more valuable? Just when I'd succeeded in creating something I wanted, I was plummeting, preparing for the 'bad' that my mental black spot was insisting lurked just around the corner.

It was now obvious that my mind was clogging with Ego distress signals. Having moved my energy out of Existence and into Life and RealLife, Ego felt abandoned, having lost control somewhere en route. I'd initiated out of a long-standing arrangement and my Ego was now trying to stop any additional acceleration by flooding my mind with a mixture of negativities and diversions. Moving away from struggle and into conscious choice had only emphasized the progress I was making. Even though I hadn't felt I'd come close to my Higher Self yet, I knew the increasing opposition from Ego meant I couldn't be too far away.

I felt a sudden shiver of purpose, a wave of urgency; not to get away from my Ego but to reconnect with the joy and fulfillment I'd felt earlier. I decided to lighten up and get back on the road. I visualized a sign saying 'Illumination City - 10km'. This became my new destination.

Starting the engine, I made a pact with Nature, promising to leave my anxiety attack behind me, disappearing in the rear vision mirror.

Meeting the intangible

My new vehicle of progress felt encouraging and I was confident I was headed in the direction of fulfilment rather than stumbling around in a post-initiation daze. The flowful nature of creating from the Heart was becoming more and more obvious, even tangible. The old way of fear, struggle and denial was dissolving away. Now I just wanted it to stay that way.

Intuition told me the next step was to open my Heart even wider and ask for more help and connect even deeper with the weird and the wonderful. The next meeting I wanted to create was with my Higher Self. It was time to clarify our connection and the part I would play in it. The only problem was, how would we meet? Was it simply a question of going with the flow and seeing who I ran into? Did I make the first move or allow it to happen? Was there something particular I had to do before this could happen? Some other initiation perhaps?

These new questions required my undivided attention. I decided to take a break from driving and pull off the road. If I was supposed to expect the unexpected, was it wrong to want my Higher Self to be a brilliant figure in white that would materialize out of thin air and change my Life forever? Or was my imagination running into Ego distortion? Perhaps Higher Self was just another ordinary Mr or Mrs Average with all the remarkable and unlimited contained inside, no obvious displays or contrived situations.

God, this was complicated! More importantly there wasn't any Truth Rush. I was back to thinking inside the cube. When was I going to leave the limits of Existence in my past? I smacked the steering wheel in frustration and an answer rebounded.

Higher Self wasn't any of those people. Higher Self didn't have a form. Form was limited. Flow was unlimited. If Higher Self wanted to support me into becoming less limited then there was no real point in meeting me in form. This would only endorse my current state, even in this weird landscape.

So, if I wanted to meet my Higher Self, I really did need to free my mind. Higher Self was helping me trust more by having no form. It was getting me out of the conditioned beliefs that physical form was more trustworthy or credible or real.

Simple. If I wanted a meeting, all I had to do was ask and then be prepared to receive.

"All right then," I said aloud, looking vainly in the mirror to make sure I looked my best. "I am choosing to meet with my Higher Self." I sat back in the seat, almost bracing myself. Nothing happened. "I am choosing to meet with my Higher Self," I repeated.

I felt a rush of truth and emotion flood my body. I dissolved into floods of tears, not of sorrow but of joy.

"Welcome back to us. I was wondering when you'd get back in touch. What took you so long?" said a gentle upbeat voice, in my head, Heart and in the car. "How are you adjusting to the connection?"

I opened my mouth to reply but nothing came out. Reconnecting with my Higher Self had been so simple but so overwhelming. All I could do was cry. I felt like one of those over-emotional people who cry at any opportunity. How embarrassing.

At last the tears subsided. "I'm really happy to be back in conscious contact, just didn't expect to be feeling like this. I thought I'd be on cloud nine, not dissolving in tears."

"Well, that's the magic of the unlimited—you know that in your Heart. Look on the bright side—it'll never get boring!" said the voice reassuringly.

"No, I can see that," I hastened." Just never thought I'd have such a tangible experience of loving support. I'm obviously really out of practice when it comes to receiving." My tears became gulps of laughter as I ventured a joke. "You're not at all what I thought—you're taller!"

"Light tends to go a long, long way here. That's the benefit of being beyond the limits of time and space!" said my Higher Self, cradling the words in a smile.

"No, seriously, how come you are so tangible and funny when you don't have a form."

"Humor isn't restricted to form you know. It's pretty handy in RealLife too. The laughter lube is always of service on all levels and service is my focus. I'm the hired help!"

"So you're funny and formless so you can be all things to all men and women."

"More a question of service. I can help you be all things to all aspects of yourself. But that's enough about me, what do you think of me?"

"This is just one enormous laugh."

"Yes it is," said my Higher Self knowingly, "more than you know. Anyway, did you want to discuss anything specific or do you want to continue this later? I'll still be here or there. Whichever way you look at it, you understand, it'll be later in your terms."

"This is so odd. I had so much I wanted to ask you but now my mind has gone blank." I felt awkward.

"Good. Try and let it stay that way!" joked my Higher Self. "If you want my advice, take a walk in the trees over to your left. Hold the intention of balance in your Heart and let Nature support you in finding your center. I'll be right with you; not watching you, you understand, just being." The voice faded, but the mere thought of my Higher Self called the presence back.

"Do you have a question?" asked the voice.

"No, just one last thought. You're incredibly responsive," I replied.

"Yes. This is one of the benefits of the acceleration with which you've been working. The greater the acceleration, the more immediate and dynamic our relationship."

"Thanks," I whispered.

"You can just speak in your Heart, that's loud enough," added my Higher Self.

"Received and understood," I mimed.

I parked the car and walked into the woods that lined the road. The late afternoon sun focused spotlights of gold between the tree trunks. The wood warmed wherever the shimmering rays fell. I sat on the ground and asked for balance, wondering how it would come to pass. "What? No thunderbolts or gold dust? No host of angels or talking unicorns?" I teased my Higher Self.

"Is that what you want?" replied my Higher Self in a booming, Thor-like tone.

"No, no. Only joking," I replied quickly, realizing the responsibility of what I'd just said.

"Good. Just clarifying what you *really* want. Besides, I don't have any spare thunderbolts or unicorns at the moment; you'll have to wait until I restock!"

The remaining part of the day was charged with purpose. As I returned to the car I felt I'd created a day when I'd made a genuine breakthrough, spending more time in RealLife than ever before. I was filled with energy and spent nearly all evening asking my Higher Self questions.

"You were the voice I heard when I started on this intensive, just after I left Michael."

"Yes, I was. I'm surprised you can remember that long ago."

"It was only this morning."

"Yes in linear perspective that's correct but in higher awareness it's a world away from now, such is your progress."

"Do you ever say anything that isn't supportive and uplifting?"

"No, but all that is communicated is a matter of perception… in the eye of the beholder as it were. All may be of service but considering it as supportive and uplifting might not always be your first choice," replied my Higher Self wisely.

"I couldn't imagine arguing with you."

"Well don't then."

"You're the perfect imaginary friend for adults!" I laughed.

"Perhaps, but there's no need to limit yourself. The Higher Self is a friend to all, irrespective of age. You don't need to be adult to get connected. Often, younger individuals are much more conscious and spiritually mature than their linear elders."

"Just listening to you, it's both amazing and sobering to realize how much limiting conditioning has embedded itself in every thought I have."

"Think of it more that your thought constructs have been created with limiting awareness. You are already learning how to construct other less-limited thoughts with much more flexibility. All it takes is practice."

"Well, it's great to have a partner in..." I paused "... creation, rather than crime! Sometimes it's really hard to know whether you're choosing from Ego or Heart."

"Well that's why you're here, so you can discern the difference. And is that your time? Well if you haven't any more questions, I'll be off," said my Higher Self, sensing my descent into sleep. I wanted to protest but couldn't.

"Rest well. There's a blanket on the back seat if you want it."

Being the boss

I was shattered the next day. Instead of getting up with the sunrise, I summoned all my energy, turned over and went straight back to sleep. It was mid morning when I next awoke and, feeling I might be missing out on something, I quickly dressed and prepared for the day's drive.

"What's the hurry?" enquired my Higher Self.

"Well, it's late and I don't want to keep you waiting; waste the day asleep. We'd better be off," I replied hurriedly.

"Don't worry or drive yourself on my account. You're the only one waiting, anyway."

"Sorry, but I don't understand," I said puzzled.

"If I were waiting, which I'm not, then I would have waited

an eternity for you to meet me here. So this morning would be but a blink of an eye; no time at all. Why are you rushing into realization when you've got all the time in the world to savor it? What's the point of traveling further and further into the future when you can learn from the present?"

"But my Ego used to say 'Hurry up, you'll be late; you need to get the maximum use of your energy and time'," I justified.

"Well linear time doesn't exist here. So perhaps, instead of racing against your conditioning, you can slow down to find out how and where you are really going. If employing your time wisely is your concern then why don't we discuss my employ? Have you written me a job description yet?"

"You want me to tell you what I want you to do?"

"Yep," confirmed my Higher Self.

I was astonished. "But isn't it meant to be the other way around?"

"No. You're the Boss, I just work here… oh yes and now."

I sat back in the car and let the silence do the talking. Nothing happened. I fidgeted as if cornered or irritated by the responsibility I was facing.

"Why have you given me such a task?" I enquired in a disgruntled tone.

"Feeling uneasy about your own power?" replied my Higher Self pointedly.

"To be honest, yes I am. I thought you were my guide, that you knew everything and I was the one learning!"

"You are learning. You're learning what your true intentions really are. When you understand them, then you'll be in the cosmic efficiency you seek. Think of this clarification of responsibility as a beginning, a way of showing your commitment. You're clarifying how you want to be helped. Nothing's set in stone you know. We can modify it later. Who knows, you might even make me redundant later."

I hesitated. "I don't think that's going to happen!"

"Fine. So focus your thoughts on how you are going to help me help you."

"Well, I want you to support me in believing in my Heart and unlimited capabilities."

"Yes, go on... I'm listening. And...?" the voice encouraged.

"And..." I continued, "...in creating from Love, not Fear; helping stabilize my physical, emotional, mental and spiritual bodies through all major restructuring. I want you to support me in appreciating that unlimited creation is natural; helping to value others and myself equally; showing me how to prevent Ego from hijacking my choices and creation capability. I want to learn the benefits of being at peace with self and environment; encouraging me to always believe that you are with me, even when I reject your advice or resist change."

I paused.

"Is that it?" asked my Higher Self.

"Yes. Well, that's all I can come up with right now," I replied, certain I'd covered everything I wanted to say.

"Thank you for the details. Let me know when you want to update it. What's next?"

"We carry on up the hills."

"Wonderful," replied Higher Self. "You're the Boss."

Filled with enthusiasm and a sense of partnership, I started the engine and accelerated out onto the open road. I continued up the mountain road that had now become a track so narrow that there was barely room for two vehicles.

What had started out as a warm, bright day had now deteriorated into overcast drizzle. Hour after hour of blind bends in the wet seemed to be conspiring to make this section of the journey a real slog. The worsening conditions brought lapses in concentration and drowsiness. I finally pulled off the road and stopped the car.

Getting out to stretch my legs seemed a good idea but

when I closed the car door, I saw how close I was to the edge of the road. I felt a spasm of fear and vertigo. It was getting late and with no villages, towns or houses en route, I realized I was going to have to spend another night sleeping in the car. Before, the lack of comfort hadn't bothered me, but now I began to long for a wide motorway and a comfortable bed.

Dampening spirits mixed with a hint of self pity was just the invitation Ego required to start niggling its way back into my mind. Reconnecting with my Higher Self, I had been occupied within my Heart center, leaving Ego to its own devices. Now that I had met my first major fear barrier, my fledgling awareness was put to the test.

Ego clearly wanted to get back into my good books. I began to hear its persuasive logic beginning to overtake my flagging trust. "Maybe it wasn't such a good idea to leave all that stable influence of Existence behind. You've got nothing against Ego; it used to be the most important part of your research. So why don't you take a fresh look at this situation. Maybe Ego can help? Ego wasn't giving you an ultimatum — Higher Self, or Ego. You're opening up to all forms of help, after all. Perhaps it was rash of you to take so many of your resources out of Existence. Maybe Ego could give you some ideas about this struggle portion of the journey; come along for the ride; someone to talk to. All this no-form, unlimited stuff was great but what about some good old fashioned company? Your Higher Self couldn't make sure you didn't fall asleep at the wheel. You need someone to help you share the burden, maybe share some of the driving. Wouldn't you like someone in form, similar to you, to keep you company? It might get very lonely talking to thin air."

Ego was becoming more confident and comfortable in my mind. "What do you think?" it pressed.

My Higher Self had gone quiet many miles before. I could feel its presence in my Heart, along with a twinge of guilt about wanting someone else in the car. But why shouldn't I enjoy some company? My Higher Self was great but it wasn't like having a passenger. This small interlude had conjured up the hope of meeting someone like me, on a journey of exploration.

Much to my surprise and delight, around the next bend there was a hitchhiker thumbing a lift. 'This is fabulous,' I thought. 'I really am able to create what I want, just like that.'

Two's company, three's a crowd

The hitchhiker was a slim, dark-haired man with a weather-worn charm, deep brown eyes and a five o'clock shadow. We were equally glad to see one another. I was bored and lonely; he appeared tired and disillusioned.

"Where are you going?" I asked, winding down the window.

"Anywhere but here. Can I have a lift?" he asked with a charming desperation.

"Of course." I lent over to open the passenger door. "Get in," I gestured.

The hitchhiker got in, clutching a guitar case and a small faded rucksack. Visibly glad for the lift, he smiled and relaxed, getting into the back seat and stretching his feet out as if he were in some luxurious armchair.

"Been alone long?" he asked as I pulled back onto the road.

"A couple of days," I replied. "To be honest, I'm glad of the company. What are you doing in the middle of nowhere?" I was inquisitive.

"I'm headed for the town on the other side of the hills. This is the only road so I thought I'd take a chance, catch a lift. I was beginning to give up back there; the novelty of all this green was really wearing thin. Still, back on track now," he grinned as his confidence began to return.

In the conversation that followed, the hitchhiker told me all about his ambitions, talents and just about everything he'd ever done. It was a lot of doing. Instead of conversing, his endless descriptions of accolade and achievement turned what had promised to be a stimulating conversation into an Ego publicizing monologue.

Focused on my driving, I decided to strike up an internal conversation with my Higher Self before the noise of the hitchhiker became deafening. "This wasn't what I wanted at all. How should I get rid of him?" I complained to my Higher Self.

"It isn't that simple. This isn't a consumer society where you can just throw away anything that you don't like. You're recycling, remember? You won't be able to relinquish your experience, much less recycle it into something new, if you haven't learnt anything. You'll just get stuck in it... which could get quite wearing."

"Oh, I don't want that. 'Captain Charisma' is wearing thin already and it's only been a couple of hours."

"Okay, it's time for an honesty pill. Open wide!"

"But I don't understand. Why have I invited my Ego back? I only wanted some company; I didn't want it to be my Ego."

"Go back to the heart of your creation. What was the intention behind what faces you now? There is a reason for everything." My Higher Self paused as if waiting for me to fill in the blanks but my mind had yet more blanks.

"I'm still confused," I admitted. "Either this is too much honesty for me or I'm missing the point. I still don't understand why, when I wanted to create company, I created it in the form of Ego? Please illuminate," I asked, with a mixture of irritation and eagerness.

My Higher Self took what appeared to be a very deep breath and continued.

"You invited Ego back because you feared being alone.

Your own company and mine wasn't enough comfort for you. Ego has successfully convinced you that you aren't good enough for yourself. Quite an achievement, wouldn't you say?"

Such immediate clarity stung me, but it was true. I'd created from fear instead of supporting myself with love. Hence why I was currently saddled with the Ego I thought I'd left far behind. The glow of realization appeared to welcome my Higher Self back into the conversation.

"See what you can learn from your companion. Everything is learning, nothing is wasted. Remember, in order to re-cycle what used to be in Limitation, you are required to go through it for a few moments, call it reminiscence of what you used to do and be. This is the process. You are going back through the need and fear of losing companionship so that you can see what a great friend you are to yourself and that friendship, like anything else in this world, is part of your learning. This process helps you clear any belief that creates a limited experience. After you've completed this phase you will be less likely to choose to form friendships because you fear being alone. You'll value and respect friendship and want to have company because you want company, not because you are frightened or bored with yourself. No more marriages of convenience with Ego, eh?"

"No I suppose not. So Ego is just showing me the type of company I create when I'm being needy."

"Yes. You were bound to meet sooner or later. It's all part of your progress forward. It's a bit like the fairground — you're viewing and experiencing distortions from the past you. Ego is just demonstrating the motivations behind how you used to create," my Higher Self concluded with a whimsical gasp of excitement.

"Thanks," I said aloud, forgetting I wasn't talking to the hitchhiker.

The hitchhiker stopped in mid-sentence. "Thanks for what?" he asked.

"All your amazing stories," I said quickly, faking a smile in my rear vision mirror.

As dark descended, the hitchhiker asked if it would be okay for him to sleep in the back seat of the car. I agreed, happy to end our conversation and get some much needed rest and silence that I now longed for.

Silence is golden

The next morning I was greeted by a cold draft as I woke from a disturbed sleep, feeling heavy-headed and lethargic. The door of the car was open and the hitchhiker was outside, brushing his teeth and being my alarm clock all in one. He gave me a wide grin, complete with toothbrush and paste, then turned back to spit into the view. I massaged my stiff neck and forced cramped legs to carry my protesting heaviness out into the morning.

"Did you sleep alright?" I asked.

"Like a baby," said the hitchhiker.

"Do you want to help out with the driving today?" I asked.

"Not now. Maybe a bit later. I thought I'd provide today's entertainment and get some rehearsing in before we get back into town."

"Well, I'd appreciate your help at some point," I replied without hiding my agitation.

"Okay," he said, sensing my irritation. "Let's get this show on the road."

It was mid morning when we finally got back on the road. Though I was glad to be moving forward, I was puzzled as to why I felt like I was dragging a lead weight. It didn't take me long to work it out. The hitchhiker decided he'd prefer to sit in the back of the car playing his guitar while I played chauffeur until lunchtime.

"Any requests?" asked the hitchhiker.

"Oh, something cheerful and uplifting," I replied.

"Okay, how about this?" he smiled broadly as I glanced into the rear view mirror.

What followed confirmed without a doubt that my definition of uplifting and his definition of uplifting were obviously two deeply contrasting concepts. He sang what sounded like a mixture of sad ballads and protest songs, trying to disguise the fact that he only knew three chords and about as many lyrics. Unfortunately I wasn't fooled, but after forty five minutes I wished I were! To inject some life back into the external monotony, I returned to the inner conversation with my Higher Self, eager to discover some purpose within my flagging experience.

"What can I do to keep my irritation in check?" I asked.

"Be at peace," came the answer.

"Well, that doesn't sound very proactive," I contested.

"Sometimes the greatest action is non-action. Allow your creation to transform. It wasn't so long ago you really wanted company. Do you know what you really want now?"

"Well, I'm definitely more able to appreciate your company and my own, now. So I'd like to drop the hitchhiker off." I was sure about this.

"Create it, then. But remember, you can't achieve it through conflict; only peace can conclude this episode. Now you understand what is in your Heart, allowing your experience to transform will create the change you're after. Trust the process. To go through your resistance without getting stuck in it is to recycle it. You're open minded and flexible, it's a doddle. I'll go. You've got incoming…" the words were nodding towards the hitchhiker.

"Hey," demanded the hitchhiker, "what did you think of that last set?"

I was startled by his demanding tone. "To be perfectly honest, I was watching the road and I wasn't really listening."

"Well..." he responded, as if giving a critique, "you weren't watching that intently because we came really close to the edge a couple of times."

My nerves were frayed as it was. I felt a surge of anger through me. I raised my voice in frustration. "Well, if I was that close, why didn't you tell me?"

"Hey, I didn't want to get you more stressed. You just need to calm down," he replied in an appeasing tone, realizing he'd struck a nerve.

"I'm not stressed," I said unconvincingly, "just a little preoccupied. Anyway, if you're going to drive from back there you might as well come up front and take over."

"No thanks, I've got loads more songs to run through. No worries, you'll be fine. We'll be reaching the top of the hills soon. You can take a break there," he said with feigned concern.

There was an outbreak of laughter in my Heart; my Higher Self had exploded into giggles.

"What's so funny?" I felt my irritation now spreading in the direction of my Higher Self.

"Well, you've got to laugh, it's so ironic! You so wanted company to share your journey with, and now your fear has created someone to take it over while refusing to take responsibility for it!"

"Very funny! Ha, ha," I retorted. "You're meant to be my friend. What kind of guidance is this?" I was taking the observation very personally.

My Higher Self ignored this provocation, continuing, "Go on, laugh! It'll do your Heart good. It's times like these when laughter lube can work wonders. Where's your sense of humor? Aren't friends meant to laugh together? Don't worry, not all company is this draining, just that which is born of fear," concluded my Higher Self fading into silence.

I stopped resisting the obvious ridiculousness of my predicament and felt immediate relief. The release of tension brought my Higher Self back,

"If you resist him, he'll stay even longer. Let the Universe help you create an alternative, something inspired consciously from love. It's easy. You know you can do it."

Just then, the hitchhiker nudged my shoulder.

"I think we should stop."

My fragile calm was flooded with anger. I was just about to yell at the hitchhiker 'You're All orders and no responsibility!' when I paused mid-sentence, substituting a fiery rejection for a complete verbal U-turn.

"Yes, why not?" I agreed. "What a great idea."

There was a parking place just up ahead and I was on the verge of pulling in when I saw the top of the range only around the next bend.

"I'll just continue to the next bend and then we'll be on the top of this world!" I could hardly believe what was coming out of my mouth.

"Wonderful," agreed my passenger.

I felt sure that I had averted a lengthening of my time with the hitchhiker by keeping my cool. Getting to the summit of this particular range had been exhausting even with the car. It was the perfect reflection of carrying Ego for one full day.

I got out of the car, went towards the edge of the viewing bay and embraced the space. The heat of the day had passed and there was now a gentle blanket of haze, giving the view candy-floss softness as far as the eye could see. A patchwork quilt of agriculture ended in a man-made border of glass and steel shining in the distance. This must be the city the hitchhiker had been referring to.

I caught a breath of surprise as I turned around to see another car pull into the bay. I hadn't seen any other vehicles in either direction for at least a day. It seemed like this hatchback had appeared out of nowhere. Curious, I turned and walked towards the new arrival.

The hitchhiker was already forming a welcoming committee at the second car, conversing enthusiastically with a woman in her late twenties who was obviously taken with his roguish charm. As I approached them the hitchhiker took something out of his rucksack and offered it to her. She accepted the gift willingly and then turned towards me as I introduced myself and asked the nature of her journey.

"Oh, I'm from over the other side of the river. I'm heading to the city for supplies," she explained.

"So it's all downhill from now on then," I replied, attempting a joke.

She smiled politely. "Yes, the road's much better from now on. Still, the view is worth the climb."

"Yes," I agreed. "It's…"

But the hitchhiker interrupted as if he'd found his cue… "So, you're going to the city, are you?" he said quickly, as if anticipating opposition. At her nod of confirmation, he went on. "Well then, would you mind giving me a lift?" He shot a sideways glance in my direction.

"I don't see any problem, if that's alright with your friend," she said, hesitating and gesturing towards me.

I tried to conceal my delight. But it was as though he could feel my disbelief, and so he added, "Well, I can stay and keep you company if you need me." The offer was full of the hope of rejection.

"Oh no," I said. "Don't worry about me. I'll be quite all right on my own. It's good to be with yourself from time to time; quiet time, a chance to catch up with what's really important."

"Are you sure?" he queried. "You were pretty down in the dumps when you picked me up."

"I'm sure," I replied, trying to keep a straight face. "Thanks for your concern."

"Are you in a hurry to get to the city?" I asked the lady driver.

"Oh, not really," she answered.

"Well, if you don't mind, I'll get moving, create a gap, then we won't have each other's fumes to contend with."

"Good idea," she said, registering my consideration while looking at her aging car.

"Have you got everything?" I asked the hitchhiker.

"Yeah," he said checking his guitar and rucksack. "Well, see ya then," he smiled meekly, trying to conceal his relief.

"Bye. Have a good trip," I said, trying to disguise my overwhelming desire to start cheering and jumping up and down on the spot.

When I left the summit I felt a rush of joy and achievement. It was as though the car was a tonne lighter. It was almost as if the car had changed capacity. Maybe that was possible here. Leaving what I now recognized to be a part of Ego perception behind gave me an immense feeling of liberation. I'd managed to recycle my need and create an alternative. I could now appreciate why the type of inner company I had was so precious and that external silence really was golden, right here, right now.

My Higher Self was still laughing and, for the first time since the beginning of my journey, I understood completely why the joke was on me.

Fear in focus

Driving down the mountain was like coasting on air. The sounds and pulse of the Earth poured through the open car windows and everything flowed with a graceful ease. The city that had been so distant was now transformed from a collection of sketchy outlines into an imposing crown on the horizon. As the road dropped down into a fertile plain, the fences and furrows of cultivation defined the natural contours of the land.

'Back to civilization,' I thought.

But if everything was meant to be familiar, then why did it already feel completely different? The first areas of farmland conflicted sharply with what I had been used to. Instead of finding flourishing crops, the land radiated exhaustion and sadness. The first fields appeared tired, as if planted with memories of Existence. The foliage looked undernourished and drought-stricken. In some places the crops had failed completely and the land was left barren. I could feel tightness, a sense of restriction.

"Has my past come back to haunt me?" I asked my Higher Self. "I thought everything was improving."

"It is," my Higher Self replied reassuringly. "These are just passing reflections of how you used to create. With the awareness of ease comes the ability to release struggle and lack more readily. You are simply looking at your past. This is a tangible summary of the Old Age—the Piscean Age. It's always been part of your world. It hasn't changed, it's just your perception and response to it that has changed. Now you know it and can feel different. When you were in Existence, this is mostly the environment that surrounded you. "

"So how long is this agricultural flash-back going on for?" I queried.

My Higher Self ignored me, instead flowing into an intense narrative. "Once upon a linear time, at the dawn of change, Researchers believed that they could beat the Ego at its game of fear by embracing self-responsibility and exchanging survival fear for the creative empowerment of choice. All that was necessary was to translate this belief into action, and then into reality. Unfortunately, thinking it and being it were two very different worlds. The jump from simple survival to the power of choice proved too great. A middle ground of 'collective responsibility' was created instead.

"Ego still remained in control, but the nature of choice was beginning to surface. Researchers thought they could clarify the power of choice by grouping together to form structures that would embody the 'greater good.' Those who understood choice would lead the way, help other Researchers mature into the understandings that would culminate in a world built of choice and individual responsibility. Struggle, pain and difficulty would be replaced by balance, ease and flow.

"Ego, however, had no intention of supporting this long term goal of individual power and responsibility. The commitment of the researcher began to be diluted, manipulated and distorted through Ego. Material security became more important than creative exploration and the accumulation of research. Ego blurred and compromised knowledge, wrapping it more and more tightly in the scarcity of linear time until it was scattered between the past, the now and the future. The researchers ability to convert their learning into wisdom became harder and harder. Confused and disorientated, Ego steered what was now known as religion, government and society into the Piscean Age. Ego flavored this world with the promise of responsibility and choice but appeared to alienate or discredit anyone who chose to actually make it their reality." My Higher Self paused as if anticipating my question.

"But if change is the only constant in the Universe then surely Ego knew this couldn't go on forever."

"Yes. In truth, evolution is always a matter of choice, never a matter of time. Linear Time is the way Ego has strung out its Existence. You know you can spend many years studying and yet have no insight to share. But in a moment of Now you can see an eternity of wisdom."

"So linear time is what has held back Researchers from bringing their energy and choices fully into Life and/or RealLife?"

"Indeed. It has constituted one of the most important limits in the whole of Limitation. How many individuals did you know in your past who believed their creations were not independent of Linear Time? How many instead believed they were running out of time from the day they were introduced to it?"

"All," I admitted.

"This is why, to build a world on choice and responsibility, Linear Time must stay in your dissolving past. Don't measure your progress by it. Don't compete with it. Don't link your moments to it. And certainly don't believe for one moment you are running out of it. Life is never too short for those who value it instead of measuring it."

I was dumb struck with this simplicity.

"Shall I continue?" queried my Higher Self, sensing my rapidly overloading mind.

"Please do. I'm just adapting."

"So to answer your question, your past has caught up with you because it is the fuel of your present progress. You are relinquishing what no longer serves you. The fear fabric of Ego, the lack, control, and scarcity of imbalance are all being recycled. All the Transformations you have just undergone have simply brought you to another period of Transmutation. Your vehicle can't run on empty, you know."

"But how can such lack and sadness be fuel?" I insisted.

"It is all fuel. You aren't going towards Ego, you are flowing through it, recycling it as you go. That is why pausing and recognizing your insights and changes in perspective is so important. Your greatest destination, the return to RealLife, will bring you beyond it completely. It is only your Ego perception that is clouding you from seeing the Transmutation. The lack within the landscape that appears to be flowing past your windows in the opposite direction is a great achievement, something to celebrate. It is your lack that is falling away from you, not your abundance. You once thought that society — built on fear and the giving up of responsibility — was the very foundation of your world. Now you see what it truly represents — just a part of your journey, but not the chosen destination. You are not in harm's way and there is nothing wrong."

"Yes, I suppose so," I mused. "It just feels so wasted, sad and disused. There is such loss here."

"This is the repetitive nature of Ego, trying to stop you moving on, creating emotional hooks to retard your progress. You feel guilty or sad and that produces a hook." My Higher Self paused. "Do you want to continue the conversation or would you rather stop?"

"No, I choose to continue," I replied demonstrating a heightened sense of resolve.

"The crops that appear to be undernourished and disease-ridden didn't seem like that when you were in Existence," my Higher Self continued, "it was normal. That which you see now didn't register or provoke those feelings because there was nothing to compare it with. All these crops are a reflection of lack, pain, struggle and imbalance. They are Ego's imbalance with environment, not the natural order. This is Ego's nature expressed through human order. There is nothing of Nature's true nature here.

"As you allow these feelings to pass without getting caught up in Ego, you are allowing your perception to change and to choose a different landscape. Once released, this area will return to the natural cycle of the unlimited. Nothing will be wasted, all will regenerate into abundance. Allow the old to die into rebirth. It's only a matter of choice rather than of time. When the memories, thought forms and beliefs you see displayed here cease to be thought, then the experience of them will stop. Their existence in this form will no longer be necessary or possible." My Higher Self fell silent.

"Go on. I am still listening," I replied, upset at the notion that I might have seemed to have lost interest. "It's just a big adjustment. I'm doing my best. Now I don't have any time, there's no reason why I can't get through this and understand it in a moment."

"Indeed. So that's enough background and foreground. Now to the practical. It's time to go and explore; test out your new understandings. Leave the car on the side of the road and walk through the fields that surround you. Allow yourself to feel what they represent. Don't resist what they are or you will be resisting your own progress."

I sat in the car, stretching Linear Time to breaking point with some abundant procrastination. My Higher Self's last sentence sounded pretty ominous. I didn't want to move. I felt like I'd reached my change threshold for today.

"Remember what I said," came the reply. "Linear Time has nothing to do with how much you can change. And by the way, you haven't reached any saturation point in your own personal changeability. If you had, this wouldn't be happening."

"But do I *have to*?" I whinged, becoming uncomfortable at the realization I'd hit a big wall of resistance.

"No. All is choice. You know that. You needn't force yourself to do anything but you could choose to F-A-C-E your experience. After all you aren't a victim of your surroundings... or are you?" This was the perfect verbal incentive. My Higher Self was getting very good at showing me how much better it knew me than I did!

I stopped arguing, took my jacket off the back seat and put it on before getting out of the car. Why was I doing that? It wasn't cold. It was as if I were attempting to protect myself from the past. Or was it the future? I shook my head. How ridiculous was that?

I began to walk. The first field I came to was a field of corn that appeared to be drought-stricken with large areas of parched soil dominating what crop was left. There was a large sign at the only entrance gate I could see. It read 'Controlled Area. Keep Out'. Although the words shouted a strong warning, the sign looked like it would fall down with one passing breeze. I climbed over the gate and headed towards the perimeter of the crop. All I had to do was feel what it was like to be in the field for just a few moments and then I could leave.

As soon as I got near the first row of corn I felt sick, wanting to turn around and run out as fast as I could. But instead I halted, as if rooted to the spot. The Ego I thought I had successfully left behind when I dropped off the hitchhiker had returned. It was convincing me with a subtle mixture of limited logic and fear that the unknown was unsupportive and dangerous. What was worse was that I was beginning to believe it.

Stalling somewhere between my Higher Self and Ego left me out in the cold. I could feel Ego clouding my thoughts and trying to take over my intention. I couldn't move forward. I wanted to know what was in store. But I knew in my Heart that I didn't need to know. The need to know was my Ego trying to take back control of my world. More to the point, there would be no room for expansion if the outcome was certain. So what was it going to be? Ever decreasing circles or unknown expansion? Or another step into the unknown? My head churned like a piece of rusty machinery. I hoped my Higher Self had had the wisdom to remain in the car but I knew this wasn't the case. It was my courage that had deserted me, not my guide.

"Do you trust yourself and your creations?" whispered my Higher Self.

"Yes," I replied.

"Then why won't you move forward?" asked the puzzled voice.

I realized that the certainty I sought was part of the illusion of control. If I knew everything that was going to happen to me, then there would be no real expansion, no experience of getting out of Limitation because I would still be reinforcing it. Expansion could only come from uncertainty. That was the buzz, the rush—the constant flow of possibility and alternatives. It was something to welcome, not to reject or smother.

I replaced control with courage and gingerly moved

further into the field. The crop didn't vary much; it appeared to have started out free of disease but a lack of water had been the main reason why the plants had withered. The crop was a reflection of a lack of flow. I'd just been through a lack of flow. Ego control had tried to convince me to stop my flow of alternatives.

"Got what you came for?" asked a voice.

"Yes Higher Self, I've got my insight. No trust, no flow!"

I turned around and retraced my steps to the edge of the field. I heard a round of applause. I turned full circle to see where it was coming from but I was alone.

"Is this your idea of a joke?" I demanded as my fear reaction downgraded to embarrassment.

"No, it's supposed to be a compliment. But if you want control back, then you can stop it instantly!" answered my Higher Self. There was silence before I replied.

"Sorry, I just felt really sensitive and I didn't know I had an audience. You caught me by surprise."

"Well, that's what letting go of fear and control is all about—surprises! Would you have acted differently if you knew you had an audience?" queried my Higher Self.

I thought hard before I answered. "My immediate response would be 'No' but that would be superficial. Not too far below the surface I do worry about what other people think of me. I would probably have tried to impress the audience, worried less and just taken the plunge." I felt a rush of energy accompany the surge of self honesty.

"So you'd be more motivated to change for others than for yourself?"

"Yes, I suppose that's true if you put it like that. I like pleasing others, perhaps more than myself."

"Do you feel the lightness that you just created?" asked my Higher Self, pausing.

"In a way," I acknowledged.

"You are unburdening yourself from your fear of the loss of approval. Quite an achievement. Want to sample more of the unknown?" enthused my Higher Self.

"Will I like it?" I answered provocatively.

"You tell me," came the churlish reply.

"If my Ego doesn't like it then it's not going to be endorsing control. Uncertainty is distasteful to Ego so that means it's expansion... right?"

"Yes, that it is," said my Higher Self. "That it is."

Fighting for protection

The next field seemed larger than all the others, probably because it was barren. The soil looked fertile enough but no attempt had been made to sow a crop. There was no gate but plenty of gaps in the fence. A weathered sign swung in the intermittent breeze reminding me of the ghost towns of the Wild West. The sign read 'Set Aside. Keep Out. By order of Government Quota'.

"What does 'Set Aside' mean?" I asked my Higher Self quizzically.

"It's the rule here. The controlling body, 'the powers that be', have decided that this area is to be set aside. The productivity here is limited. The external authorities decide what can and can not be grown. Go inside, you'll feel soon enough." This explanation did little to quell my curiosity and the apprehension that was growing in the shadows of my mind.

I lifted a weakened part of the fence and slid under it into the field. From the moment I put my feet on the soil I felt like I was being watched. I drew my coat tightly around myself, fixed my eyes on the center of the field and kept on walking. The air was thick and its stiffness repelled me as though I was walking against the flow, even though there were no visible obstacles.

"Why do I feel so drained and frightened?" I stammered.

"Well, this is the field of conflict," replied my Higher Self in a gentle but firm tone. "You feel as if there's a hidden enemy; someone or something that could take all your resources away."

"And is there?" I replied, my apprehension gaining momentum.

"You tell me." came the reply.

"Well if I don't fight then there can't be a conflict."

"Go on."

"The field is giving off the sensation of conflict because it's going completely against the natural order of creation. Growth is being held back, not because the field is regenerating or resting but because it's not allowed to produce. So it's the conflict between the forces of control and the natural flow of creation that I can feel. And there's no reason for me to start preparing for trouble or start protecting myself because that would be my environment dictating my choices. There isn't a conflict unless I choose to create one."

"Or unless your Ego draws you into one," added my Higher Self.

As I walked further, the fear became more pronounced. I looked behind me but there was nothing there. A wind began to blow strongly, first from the left and then directly in my path. Dust and fine particles of soil blew up into my face and I couldn't see. My eyes kept watering, sore with the sudden onslaught of grit. This temporary loss of vision only added to my distress. What if my physical senses were right and I should be careful? I couldn't protect myself because I couldn't see. I became frustrated with my blurred vision and even when it was restored I started to question what I'd missed or might still be unable to see. I should go back or at the very least find some shelter. What was the point in continuing? There was nothing there but a desert of anxiety full of potential danger.

My Heart was telling me to stand my ground or at least keep walking until I could honestly feel it was time to leave. The more I progressed, the more the argument between my Heart and my mind grew. 'You should take some precautions, you don't know what's over the rise.' I'd had enough. I sat down on the bare soil and called my Higher Self.

"What is going on? I feel exhausted."

"You're fighting with your Ego. Nothing too important," said my Higher Self appearing completely disinterested.

"But what if there is some truth in what I'm feeling? It seems pretty real to me."

"Sorry but I can't help you decide what is real and what isn't, that's up to you. Your truth is your own. Do you trust your Ego's assessment or your Heart's?"

"Well… my Heart of course. Ego's bound to be supporting my fear."

"So misunderstanding over? Or do you still want to take precautions, protect yourself from the wasteland?"

"Well when you put it like that it seems absurd. Why would I protect myself from something that's actually nothing—an illusion?"

"Why indeed?" replied my Higher Self wryly.

"So I've been wasting my energy," I said sheepishly, "fitting in well with my environment," I smiled.

"Yes you've been brawling with your Ego. But you can come out and face the illusion."

I stood up and looked around the empty field. There was nothing but the fence line and a few birds dust-bathing in the soil. How harmless everything looked and felt now.

"But it was all so real. I don't understand. Surely wanting to protect yourself in times of danger is normal."

"Normal to Ego, maybe," soothed my Higher Self, "but not for your Heart. Why would you choose to protect yourself? What are you frightened of? A world built on love, abundance and joy? Or a world built from pain, conflict and delusion?"

"Well there's no reason to be frightened of a world of love, abundance and joy… So I was protecting my Ego by shutting down my Heart, the result being that I was falling back into Ego and the experience of fear, denial and lack."

"Yes. And as you saw, Ego put on a pretty convincing show."

"But what was behind it? Why did I fall for it?" I really wanted to understand.

"The need to protect self is a misunderstanding that Ego delights in. It's one of its best scams. If you try to protect yourself, fearing the outside world, be it a hostile reaction, a group of depressed people or a 'bad energy' of some sort, then you are simply protecting Ego. In all your Transformations and Transmutations, you are expanding so that you can rejoin all that is loving and abundant. There is no point in barricading yourself within fear because what you truly want won't reach you. It's Ego that has hijacked your resources and tried to convince you to protect your world. No guidance that is loving, however rational or incredible it may appear, will encourage you to expand your fear."

"So how can I choose differently next time rather than fall into the need for protection?"

"Always believe that the world you are creating, co-creating with the Grand Flow, is loving and don't choose to think of anything else. Choose what's in your Heart instead of giving your Ego thoughts with which to threaten you. Look for the intention behind the action. Is it loving and supportive or is it fearful? It's always simple; it's only Ego that likes to complicate," clarified my Higher Self. "It's also worth pointing out that this experience was more intense because you are now working with more parts of yourself and you have more opportunity to accelerate…"

"Or to get bogged down," I said, finishing my Higher Self's sentence.

"*Or* get caught up in Ego. You weren't so much bogged, just tripped up a little."

"So from now on, all I'm required to do is take responsibility for what is loving and ignore what is fearful?"

"Yes. You gain the ability to tell the difference between what is self loving and supportive rather than self limiting and Ego protecting. So now do you understand why this field is called Set Aside?" asked my Higher Self with a powerful directness.

"It's a reflection of how easy it is to hold back the true nature of creation," I responded.

"Yes. In this place, governments tell people what they can and cannot grow. The system has controlled the flow of abundance until surplus is now common. And yet so much goes to waste or is created by exhausting the land. Production has become the only concern, there is no balance between production and recuperation. The intention of 'Set Aside' isn't to regenerate, it is to maintain control. The natural cycles have been manipulated to create permanent imbalances in natural resources. Here, 'more' is actually less because the 'more' is based on greed—the control of abundance."

I shivered, shocked to the very core. It seemed unthinkable that such gross mismanagement of resources could happen, let alone be normal.

"But can't this be changed?" I said feeling a sense of desperation.

"Everything in the Universe can change, it's all a matter of choice. But this is your past. Just remember from this moment that the most concentrated fertilizer you can scatter in your environment is to create from love, not from fear. Changing your inner nature is changing your outer environment. This was indeed some of the most intense fear you will feel in this passing phase. Being here saturated you with the fear of your own potency and held many conditionings that Ego had been using to protect itself against your true nature. But through wielding the power of choice, these sensations flowed through you until they were gone.

"You are no longer the person you were. You know in your Heart that this wasteland will bloom again, will regenerate and a crop of realization will grow to seed permanent change where Limitation once choked under the burden of its own constraints."

There was a deep silence. I felt like I was at my own funeral. A deep sense of struggle was over. A coffin with the person my Ego wanted me to be slid into the heart of the Earth. I'd buried vast tracts of my past.

"Shall we move on?" asked my guide.

"Please," I replied willingly.

Leaving Set Aside made me realize just how much energy was being liberated through clarifying my relationship with Ego. Instead of becoming depressed by the amount of change that I now knew lay before me, I felt a wave of gratitude and a determination to keep going.

The cereal sea

"Where to next?" I asked with renewed optimism.

"Up to you. Your choice is my command, oh learned one. I thought you might like the Genie touch," teased my Higher Self theatrically.

I didn't hear the reply. My attention had immediately been diverted when I saw the Mini parked in front of me on the right hand side of the road. I walked towards it in astonishment.

"How can the car be there when I parked it a mile down the road?" I spluttered.

My Higher Self broke into song. "Let's go round again... If I could turn back time..."

I interrupted. "Well, if I were you, I wouldn't give up the

day job!" I smirked. "I like your idea of karaoke, but what does this mean? How did the car get here?"

"Distance becomes less relevant the further you travel; less linear, more loopy," replied my Higher Self, draping a broad smile from the beginning to the end of the sentence. "The Mini is a little reminder that you never need to go back to pick up what you think you might need. Only fear is left behind. Everything that you require in each moment is always right within your grasp."

"That's comforting," I said. "I'm just going to explore the next field. Back soon,"

As I approached the field I looked for a sign; I felt curious about what would be written. My curiosity diminished as I was confronted with big red letters exclaiming 'Subsidence. Keep Out.'

There were no fences and no gates, only a strip of land with what appeared to be a relatively healthy crop of wheat. I couldn't see any subsidence. Perhaps there was an ulterior motive for scaring people away. On a sensory level I wasn't receiving anything. Perhaps this was merely an exercise in trust, a 'double-bluff' or a test after my last experience. This was, after all, the first relatively healthy crop I'd encountered.

I walked into the field and began to flow with the motion of the undulating waves through the ears of wind-swept wheat. The movement was quite hypnotic and before I knew it I had lost my sense of direction, floating in a sea of golden brown.

Suddenly, the ground shifted beneath my feet. I stumbled temporarily and then regained my balance. This time, instead of feeling fear as my first response, I stood still, determined to regain my calm. 'A touch of sea sickness perhaps,' I laughed to myself. Continuing to walk in the same direction, I came close to what appeared to be an old mine shaft. The wheat had fallen in and around the opening.

I started to feel nervous. The ground moved again and the earth fell away immediately behind me. I was trapped on the narrow strip of land between the shaft and the subsidence. My calm was sinking rapidly. Realizing that one movement could create a total landslide, I shouted for help inside myself.

"Help me, Higher Self, help me."

"Why do you doubt? You aren't in harm's way," my Higher Self responded calmly.

"You could have fooled me," I stuttered.

"Unfortunately, that is still too easy to do! Trust yourself and your doubt will stop dissolving your world. What do you see?" persisted my Higher Self.

"A field of healthy wheat," I replied.

"You wanted to find what was productive and you have. Don't let it subside into your doubts. One doubt can undo all your productivity. Commit to what you feel, not to what appears to be before you. It's a passing wave of illusion."

My intuition was telling me to move even further into the field rather than going back. I took great gulps of trust and leapt into the center of the crop. My feet were greeted by solid ground, and a whispering conformation from the golden brown sea.

"What can you believe now?" said my Higher Self.

"I can always find an alternative to fear," I replied.

"Indeed. Never doubt creation! You are what you create, it's that simple. Indecision causes more instability within your Heart and creations than you can appreciate now. So don't let doubt create weakness where, in truth, none exists. Ego will always try to blind you with a vision of fear when you are passing back through your limited conditioning. But fear comes from nowhere and goes to nowhere. It is superficial and momentary and only becomes a reality when you endorse it. Just a small shift in perception is all it takes to keep expanding. Anything is possible, so choose the anything you want, not what your Ego wants."

I walked over the hill and back down the other side of the field, pretending to swim in the motion of the wheat. I could now see and feel why control, conflict and doubt had kept me occupied in Limitation for so long. More importantly, I was beginning to appreciate why my Higher Self had led me into fear — to understand the practicalities of recycling it. Now I was out my other side, the unknown had never felt so appealing! I jumped the ditch between the field and the road expecting to find my car where I had last seen it. It was gone.

"Where's the car gone?" I asked my Higher Self. "Is this yet another surprise?"

"Bingo!" came the reply.

"Is this your idea of exercise?" I asked, half smiling.

"That depends on you. Do you want to walk?"

"No," I replied immediately.

"What do you want?" came the question.

"I want the car back," I said firmly.

"Are you expecting to get the past back again?" probed my Higher Self.

"No, but I want a car that is just as powerful or more so," I replied, refreshed by my clarity.

"Marvelous. Look over your left shoulder," said my Higher Self whimsically. I turned around to see a midnight blue convertible.

"That's gorgeous!" I exclaimed.

"It will get you to your next destination. If you believe you can handle the acceleration, it's yours."

"No doubt there," I said.

"Really?" asked my Higher Self provocatively.

"Well, no doubt that I want to focus on, put it that way! Thanks. Is this one of the benefits of the unknown?"

"You could say that. More a reflection of the Initiation you've just undergone."

"Another one? Well perhaps this is a worthy reflection of my acceleration."

"We'll see. Just remember, when you are advancing through your discoveries, nothing stays the same. Nothing." My Higher Self appeared to be landing a heavy hint.

"Okay, I'll try and remember that," I said with a departing commitment as I began to stray towards the car. The tone of my Higher Self brought me back.

"Don't try, simply remember it."

"Right. Message received and understood. I'm off to engage my new gear."

I paused philosophically. "One question before we head off: Our relationship has changed, hasn't it?"

"What do you mean?" came the reply.

"Well, it appears as though we're not as close as we were. Are you encouraging me to be more independent? To share my perspectives and truths? Or are you preparing to leave?"

"Both really," replied my Higher Self, "but not in the way you're thinking. The nature of relationship is maturing within you. No longer do you crave the approval or security of 'like.' You've gone beyond that. You don't need me to like what you are saying or who you are being; you are simply asking for guidance. Your attention is now on understanding the intention behind your creations. It isn't that there's more space between us, it's more a case of your Heart growing so there's more space for both of us and your maturing perspectives. You want unlimited creativity; well, this is part of it."

My Higher Self continued. "Think of us now as sharing a mansion whereas before you were making do with a cluttered bed-sit! And I was... well, never mind. I wasn't really a priority then; a sort of 'spiritual squatter'. But now you realize that being more in your Heart allows us to live in harmony and it manifests the perfect company and silence."

"So we're really going up in the world then," I joked, filled with a certain sense of pride.

"Well, less of Pilgrim's Pride and more of Pilgrim's Progress; expanding in all directions. Does that help you adjust?"

"Yes, thank you Higher Self. I'm really beginning to enjoy this journey, now that I've started sharing the driving. Ready to travel?" I chuckled.

"Indeed, ready... even when you don't know you are," replied my Higher Self.

"I'll take that as a 'Yes'."

With that, we sped away through the remaining countryside passing mile upon mile of lush farmland. Gradually the road became dotted with farms and small villages until finally it widened and I began to feel the pulse of the City.

A night on the town

The city beat was much more invigorating than I remembered, even addictive, in comparison to the undulating calm of the land. I immediately felt stimulated into formulating a plan. First, find a place to stay while it's still light, get some food at the supermarket, then go out on the town to explore.

Driving around to get my bearings, I came across a street packed tightly from end to end with small hotels. Each displayed a unique brand of hospitality as it competed with its neighbor. I stopped at the first one with a vacancy sign, parked the car and walked into reception.

I was greeted by a long, faded reception counter with no one behind it. I rang the desk bell and it gave off a barely audible apathetic tone and still no one came. I became impatient.

"Is there anyone here?" I called out.

Still no one arrived. I began to encapsulate myself in a cloud of impatience, frustrated by my expectations not being met and the blatant lack of service.

"How do they expect to run a hotel," I muttered, "if they aren't there to greet potential guests?"

Finally, a middle aged man shuffled from the back office to the counter. He looked exhausted, the dark patches under his eyes nearly engulfing his face. He didn't look at me, it was more through or past me.

"Can I help you?" he murmured, his face as vacant as the hotel seemed to be.

"Yes, I'd like a room for a couple of nights," I replied. "Do you have any available?"

"Yes. Smoking or non-smoking?" he continued in a low monotone.

"I'd like non-smoking," I answered curtly.

"Okay," he said reluctantly. "You can have number nine."

"Could I see it first?" I queried, no longer caring if I hide my dissatisfaction or not.

"You'll have to wait until the lady comes back from her break because I can't leave the desk unattended."

"You managed pretty well before," I muttered under my breath.

"If you just give me the key and tell me which room it is, I'll take a look myself." I stood indignantly as the man scanned me up and down like he was assessing if I was trustworthy or not. 'What is the stupid man doing? Does he think I'm going to steal the room?' I thought defensively.

"Okay," he agreed, finally handing me the key begrudgingly. "Turn left and it's the third room after the first row of cars." He motioned haphazardly out the reception doors.

"Thanks," I replied unconvincingly.

Turning left, I walked past the cars and saw a door with the number nine on it. I put the key in the lock but it stuck. I fiddled and fiddled until the lock finally gave up the fight and let me in. As soon as I opened the door, I realized I didn't want to stay. I'd been struggling ever since I arrived, becoming agitated and angry instead of simply acknowledging that I was resisting the flow of creation. Driving through the countryside only a few hours ago hadn't been a struggle, it was an enjoyable flow. I didn't have to make it work, argue, or create a drama; I knew what I wanted and creation flowed.

I quickly closed the door behind me and walked back to reception. I handed over the key.

"Thanks," I said, "but I think I'll leave it." I felt self righteous, as if his unhelpful attitude had contributed to my rejection. The man remained expressionless and simply put the key back on its hook and retraced his steps mechanically towards the back office.

I couldn't wait to leave but I couldn't understand why, when everything had been going so well, I'd suddenly become so reactive. I was facing an uncomfortable and unpleasant impasse. If I created everything in my world, how could my joy have created such an unresponsive and unfriendly receptionist? I was just about to ask what was wrong when my Higher Self replied to the thought.

"You aren't doing anything wrong, just going through a new wall of conditioning."

"But I thought I'd done that already," I protested, still processing my dissatisfaction.

"You have," said my Higher Self reassuringly. "This is just the next layer."

"So what's the wall made from this time?" I replied, unwilling to relinquish my irritation.

"Your resistance," replied my Higher Self calmly.

"What resistance?" I pleaded, feeling my petulance deflate.

"Your internal resistance. You've been wrestling with allowance ever since you arrived at the hotel. You've let your resistance take over your creativity rather than letting it pass through you the way it did when you were in the fields. It is resistance that has produced your dislike of the receptionist and the room, as well as your agitation and sarcasm. Pretty creative of Ego, but not what you want."

My Higher Self was trying to make light of my situation but I wanted to keep hold of my feeling of injustice.

"Why are you criticizing me?" I persisted. "Or is this your brand of sarcasm?"

"This isn't criticism," said my Higher Self, appearing to stand back within my Heart in the wake of my outburst, "it's observation. You have simply put all of your creativity into a myriad of resistance alternatives; divided the big block that stands in your way into a variety of smaller hurdles."

I was becoming very disgruntled. My Higher Self was soothing my mental inflammation but what seemed like a concentrated dose of criticism was simply too much. Deep down I knew that I was now hiding behind my reluctance to change my mind and thus to change my experience of my world. In the few short moments I'd been here, Ego had invested too much of my energy in judgment and anger to give it all up now.

"I'm going to the supermarket to get some food and have a change of scene. I'll come back and find a hotel later," I said, feeling a twinge of failure.

"As you wish," came the guidance. "The scene and the resistance will still be here when you get back, although it might appear to have grown."

The fear of not finding somewhere to stay started to build in my mind. I could feel my Higher Self grinning like a Cheshire cat.

"Okay, okay," I admitted begrudgingly. "You win. I was wrong to try and shut you out, to close my Heart when I know it is the only true source of guidance. I was caught in a childish tantrum."

"Well, you are no spiritual infant," smiled my Higher Self, stepping closer once more, "and there is no reason to apologize. Your perception was temporarily clouded by Ego. Just another misunderstanding."

I was silent. The last sentence was hanging in the air, both hypnotizing and overwhelming in its loving simplicity. I sat motionless in the car for what seemed an age. My stubbornness was wearing thin. The longer I remained in the car the more I could see my ignorance. I chose to recycle it with the willingness to learn.

"All right, I'm ready to convert my resistance into something helpful," I said waving an imaginary white flag.

My Higher Self took a long, wise, deep breath as if refueling, and began again with endearing warmth.

"Being in resistance to your world happens on a major or minor scale every moment of your experience. You don't like what someone says about you; you don't agree with others' decisions. You don't want to create without knowing what is going to happen; you don't want to help yourself. And so it goes on. For Ego, resistance is life itself. Ego owns this monopoly and represents its biggest manufacturing industry with products to suit all types and all tastes.

"Ego sells these products in the Supermarket of Experience. There are many different aisles, Love, Lack, Joy, and Fear to name but a few. Eventually you come to the aisle marked 'Resistance' and you get to see how varied all the products are. There is resisting yourself, resisting others, resisting your children, resisting your dreams... the aisle extends as far as the eye can see."

"So If I enter the supermarket of Life, under the influence of Ego, let's say, I will probably go straight to the aisle marked 'Resistance,' and buy more."

"Indeed. If you take your creative tantrum into the Supermarket then Ego will most likely encourage you to spend all of your available energy on products that only it can use. The bigger the outburst, the bigger the shopping spree. And the more you reinforce conditioning the more you're encouraged to put resistance on your list of essential purchases."

"So the more Ego products I buy, the less likely I am to explore the aisles related to Life because I will have spent all my resources on Ego?"

"Yes, and the more you spend on Ego the more energetically indebted you become because you aren't expanding your options, only limiting them. The less energy you have, the more likely it is you'll fall back into conditioning and buy everything for Ego and nothing for Heart. The next time you go into the Supermarket of Life you won't see anything but the aisle of Resistance. This is the point when an individual can choose to turn their back on choice permanently and become an Ego-driven victim."

"So when I encounter a wall of resistance, my environment could appear totally unsupportive only because it's my Ego trying to stop further recycling."

"Yes."

"So the greater the environmental disturbance, the greater the energy stored within the resistance. And it's only when I am able to maintain my balance under any circumstances that I won't feel any disturbance whatsoever?"

"Correct. At this stage, disturbance is a big indicator of your potential progress and ability to recycle resistance. You are learning how it feels to be in resistance and also what to do when you are within it. Before it was just another part of Existence but now you can see it as another part of your research. Resistance is, after all, only a brand of fear. But if you let your Ego talk you out of your Heart and into your mind, it will try and convince you to accept resistance as a part of normal experience, telling you there are some things that you can never change."

"What the Ego is really saying," I interjected, "is that there are parts of Ego it never wants me to change. But... Love and Change are the Nature of the unlimited and these are the only things that will never change. But I can always adjust the degree to which I allow Ego to restrict my flow of change."

"Well said. So back to our situation here at the hotel... You struggled with making your experience work instead of understanding why it wasn't what you expected. Your resistance became obvious because you didn't get what you wanted. Goaded on by Ego, you argued with all aspects you could. The result? You scattered your energy and abandoned any alternatives that you could have discovered. Ego was playing divide-and-conquer by convincing you this was an all-or-nothing situation and if you didn't get what you wanted then you should reject everything else. It became all-or-nothing instead of something in between. If you had left in your energetic huff, you would simply have carried your resistance to the next hotel and the next, slowing yourself down and making it harder to actually create what you wanted."

"So I got off the resistance merry-go-round before I spun out of my Heart and into the arms of Ego?"

"Yes."

"Okay, makes sense. So what do I do now? How can I convert my resistance into useable energy?" I ventured.

"Return to your center, find your peace and rebuild yourself. Looking with self enquiry, who were you with a moment ago? "

"My Ego... I was being pushy and condescending, neither of which I want now," I admitted.

"Go on..."

"I'll change. Stop the Ego influence, focus on what I want and believe I have all the resources I require to create it within this moment. Then my environment will change to reflect my change. My disgruntled persona will have smoothed itself out."

"Wonderful. So what are you going to do now?"

"Go in search of a hotel room," I said, starting the car.

"But why are we leaving?" asked my Higher Self quizzically.

"So I can find a room," I replied.

"But what's wrong with here?"

"I've already tried here." I rolled my eyes into the back of my head. "I'll never do that again…" I stopped mid sentence like a thief caught in the act. "I mean…" I faltered and fell silent as my cheeks warmed with a flush of embarrassment. My Higher Self gave me all the silence I needed to emphasize the realization.

"That was trying — now this is creating." My Higher Self let the words sink in.

"Fine. So if each moment is truly an unlimited creation opportunity then the past doesn't matter. What happened before can't affect what I want to create now unless I let my Ego influence me."

"Go on."

"So there's absolutely no reason why I can't go back into the same hotel and my experience of creating a room be totally and utterly the opposite of what it was when I was in resistance."

"Do you want to try out what your Heart is telling you?" hinted my Higher Self. "No all-or-nothing, no need to rush from one polarity within self to the other."

"Okay."

"So your assignment, should you choose to accept it, is to create a hotel room and recycle all previously discovered resistance." My Higher Self feigned an air of the utmost importance.

"To boldly change where I never thought I could change before — I accept."

I left the car and walked back to the reception desk for the first time, all over again. There was a dull ache in my stomach as I contemplated how many pieces of humble pie I was about to ingest. But instead of a sense of déjà vu, it was like walking into a completely different space. There was a welcoming lady in her mid thirties behind the reception desk and a fresh, efficient atmosphere.

"Do you have any rooms?" I asked, taken aback by such a changed environment.

"Certainly. What type of room where you looking for? Smoking or non-smoking? Quiet or near the pool?"

"Bright, non-smoking, quiet," my answer came readily.

"I think I have just the room for you. Number eleven. If you would like to follow me, you can take a look at it first."

Astonished at the complete turnaround, I mumbled "Yes" and followed the lady who led me out into a beautiful sunset. The room was everything I'd asked for, plus it had a small kitchen area and was much bigger than I had considered standard.

"I'll take it," I heard myself saying.

"Great," she replied. "I'll just need you to come back to reception and fill in a guest card. Number eleven is an executive room but, because the maid is off today, none of the standard rooms are ready for occupancy. Don't worry, you can have this room at the same rate as the standard. Are you just passing through?"

"Well, as a matter of fact…" I paused.

"You just came for a room" the lady echoed my words, "but Bill wasn't at reception and when he came he was unfriendly and unhelpful? Oh please don't worry about him. He doesn't seem to like anything or anyone; just like he's trying to shut the whole world out. It's a mystery why he stays at all. Just ask for me when you check out. My name is Grace."

"Thanks, Grace. You've been really helpful."

After checking in I went back to the car for my bag.

"Amazing what allowance and peace can do," I reflected. "Thank you, Higher Self. Mission accomplished. I'm feeling on top of this particular world so I'll continue my balancing act out on the town. Don't forget to dress for dinner!"

I showered, changed and decided to go with the flow. No recommendations, just spontaneity.

Living it up

All the restaurants, streets and clubs were lit up as if it was a special occasion. It seemed a garish but fun contrast after the simplicity and elegance of the natural light in the countryside. I was getting hungry, so I headed for the restaurants and bars that huddled tightly together vying for attention on either side of the riverbank.

I parked the car and walked along the banks until a group of street performers solicited my attention. I watched as one mimed his intention and the other magically created it. The magician was a better comic than he was a card smith, so the entertainment came from the ridiculous rather than the sublime. Seduced by the organic publicity, I took a table at the restaurant they were promoting and continued to watch as both Fool and Sage captured the hearts and the coins of enchanted passers by. Dinner was unusual, beautifully presented and completely satisfying. I couldn't wait to continue the evening as it had started.

Leaving the restaurant, who should I bump into but the hitchhiker. He looked both surprised and pleased to see me.

"Fancy seeing you here! Enjoying city life?" he enquired.

"Yeah, I'm having a fantastic time. This place gets my vote," I enthused, pointing at the restaurant I'd just left. "Have you got a regular slot yet?" I asked.

"Not exactly. I'm still doing a lot of street performing, but getting the odd gig too," he replied modestly.

"Well, that's something to build on," I affirmed.

"Do you want me to show you around?" he offered.

"Why not? Lead on MacDuff," I replied theatrically.

We began to walk, the hitchhiker pointing out the highlights, and lowlights, of town. "This is the heart of the night life up and down the river. It's called The Snake because of the way the river curves. This is one of my favorite bars; it's called Emerald's. Fancy a drink?"

"Love to," I answered, following the flow. "So what have you been doing with yourself" I asked, "apart from performing?"

"Not a lot actually. I managed to get a flat just off the river. I'm looking after it for someone, so that's really fortunate. I've been trying to get inspiration for some new songs." He pulled out a joint asking, "Do you want a smoke?"

"No thanks, not my scene. I'll stick to my drink." My forceful response surprised me. It was as if the whole of my body shouted NO! "One state-altering substance is enough for me. I'll be so laid back I'll fall over!" I added.

"Oh, go on. It'll help you get a new perspective on your life. You strike me as the searching type; someone looking for something greater, out of the ordinary."

"Yes, I am as a matter of fact. But how can that help me find it?"

"Well," began the hitchhiker, "it lets you expand yourself beyond your existing limitations. It gives you confidence to explore other areas of yourself. It facilitates a total mind shift; releases all your inhibitions. It stops you struggling to be you and lets you come out of yourself."

I felt uneasy as if I was going back into my previous experience of me letting the hitchhiker run my life. Why should I become dependent on something outside of myself to help me change? I was the one responsible for change. If I responded differently this time then everything would be different. I had my Heart, my intuition and my Higher Self to help me come through Ego control and that was more than enough. I stayed in my center. No falling into conflict or losing myself in the ramblings of mental justification this time.

"No thanks, I'll pass," I replied firmly.

"You don't know what you're missing," replied the hitchhiker with the hint of a challenge, taking a long drag on his joint and blowing smoke and then smoke rings in my face.

At that moment I felt all of the momentum of the evening ebb away as if it were draining down an imaginary plughole in the center of the bar. The conversation diverted into vortices of repetition. The street lights flashed on and off, the people ran around in a frenzy, the room started spinning. I felt sick. If this was even close to what I was supposed to be missing I wanted nothing to do with it.

"So is there any inspiration blowing your way? Any revelations?" he asked.

"The revelation is that there aren't any great revelations for me! Everything appears to have become disjointed," I mumbled.

"Hey that's a good one: disjointed. You've been dis—jointed. You're sure you don't want to become a comic?" laughed the hitchhiker, pouting his lips and skillfully blowing another perfect smoke ring.

"No, seriously, I feel really tired. I think I'll call it a night," my voice flattened.

"Oh, don't leave now, the night's young. You haven't even given the party a chance to get started. There's loads more places to go; we can keep going until the early hours."

"No, I'm really tired," I persisted. "My only pub crawl is going to be the crawl from Emerald's to the car. Besides..." I left in mid sentence without answering the hitchhiker's other objections.

I felt really fragile but didn't know why. Surely I could have a little fun without collapsing into a heap? I walked the full length of the river and back down the other side towards the car. By that time I was sure I could find the hotel. But I was wrong. I drove another twenty minutes before I noticed a sign saying 'Dickens Street.' When I finally arrived in my room, I was overcome with fatigue and confusion, took off one shoe, and began to take off my clothes, falling asleep in the process.

———   ———   ———

The next morning I awoke to the sound of someone drilling in my head and my Higher Self shouting in my right ear.

"Good Morning!" my Higher Self boomed jovially. "Big night last night?"

"Yes," I replied meekly. "Please don't shout. I'm having enough trouble contending with the drill."

"Well, you hired it," came the reply.

"Yes but there's no need to remind me." My head started throbbing even more. "Look, Higher Self, if you're walking around in there, can you please sit down!" I pleaded.

"That's your Ego in the office of your mind. I'm in your Heart," came the lightning response.

"Ouch," I grimaced. "There's no need to prod me. I forgot for a moment. But how about a little compassion?"

My Higher Self was silent.

"Is that silent compassion?"

My Higher Self nodded.

"Fine... Compassion doesn't have a volume control, it just is. So is that why you were so quiet last night? Or did you decide to leave me to my own devices?" I was beginning to come to what I could safely say were my limited senses.

"I was there with you, just on a different wavelength. You'd tuned in to a different frequency; tuned out so actually you couldn't hear me." My Higher Self paused to soften the tone. "Feeling a little insecure? Didn't trust yourself last night, eh?"

"Yes, guilty as charged. Last night wasn't a good time to trust myself with myself but at least I quit when I was ahead! I didn't go completely out of balance," I lamented.

"Don't be harsh on yourself. You haven't done anything wrong, you were simply doing the practical part of your assignment, exploring the entertainment in your world. Your experiences are always the product of your intentions. What was your intention last night?"

"To have a good time." I paused. "But I think my definition of a good time has changed. Perhaps that was the source of my confusion. I went to a place to enjoy something and at first I did. But when I continued and tried some variations, it was as if the joy wouldn't stretch and so it started to dissolve. Going to the bar was like turning a corner and expecting to feel more of the same but I didn't. I felt less of the same, and then my experience started to evaporate. What really happened?"

"You went beyond your joy, against your heartfelt wish and into imbalance and then into extreme. You were like a pendulum passing the point of balance and then accelerating out into extreme. But there is nothing wrong. You are simply more aware of balance and how you feel when you go past it. As you said: your definition of a good time has changed. But look on the bright side—you've got some very valuable research. How can you understand contrast until you've straddled the Great Divide?"

"Talking of which," I interrupted, "the first Great Divide I'd like to bridge is the one going through the center of my head. Have you got anything for a hangover?"

"Drink water," replied my Higher Self with a motherly practicality. "You've dehydrated yourself."

I gulped down two large glasses of water and immediately felt better.

"Well, that worked a treat," I gasped. "Thanks."

"Don't mention it. Now, as we were both saying…" The

guidance was gushing enthusiastically towards the next sentence.

"You're in a chatty mood this morning," I interrupted again. "Just let me get comfortable and then you can elucidate all you want." I filled all the glasses I could find with water, just in case I had a relapse. I lay down on the bed, propping myself up with all the pillows, giving out waves of ease signaling my readiness to absorb the incoming guidance.

"Well," began my Higher Self, "as you recycled your way back through all the different levels and types of resistance, your Ego invited you to start playing the game of self denial. It looks quite harmless on the surface but the longer you play this particular game, the more addictive it becomes. Self denial goes hand in hand with doubt and can become all-consuming in a matter of moments. The more it's endorsed, the more confined the Heart becomes and the less you can hear me. You think I ignored you last night but in fact it was the other way around. You chose to stop listening and trusting yourself. You stepped out of your Heart, past joy and spontaneity, and swung out of balance. Fortunately you stopped before you gave Ego complete control. The hitchhiker was enticing you into greater and greater Ego control but you were able to choose non-conflict and move on. A maturing use of insight. Well done."

"Thanks for the compliment. What I want to know is, how did it all drain down the plug hole so quickly? One moment everything was great, the next minute it was all over."

"Self denial is a game of one, run by Ego. How you get into denial doesn't matter; how you react when you are there is what's important. Whether you've chosen to escape, suppress or depress, the result is the same. You play with Ego's rules and disallow any other input from the outside or inside worlds. You believe it's pointless letting anyone else into the game because they just wouldn't understand it, and you certainly don't want to share it with anyone else because then it wouldn't be exclusive. So as soon as you shut out other alternatives, it was just you and Ego."

"So it's back to the pendulum; I was swinging around my center. But when all that energy was released and recycled, the oscillations of the pendulum got bigger and bigger until I was spending my energy at the extremes instead of flowing with balance. I swung straight past balance and just kept on going."

"Yes, but yesterday was the first time you'd achieved so much recycling. And also bare in mind that you'd gone from a purely feminine energy environment to a masculine energy one, and that contrast also contributed to your extreme behavior. Don't worry, there is nothing wrong. All you experienced was how quickly your Ego could take advantage of you even when you thought you were reducing its effect on you. Ego concentration might have reduced with your insights but Ego can still seize control when you start to accelerate due to all your new recycled fuel."

"So it's not enough to complete the Initiation, it's also important to maintain balance so that I can creatively use what I've recycled or Ego will try and use it against me."

"Rather, Ego will use it to reinforce Ego; get you back where Ego thinks you belong. Self denial is such a powerful Ego tool because it is totally controlled by Ego with a single objective: to turn you away from any aspect of Life that might cause expansion. The recipe is simply Ego plus a subtle dash of avoidance and a pinch of self sabotage. Leave to simmer and then it's easy to convince Self that this game is useful; that it preserves energy and protects you from destructive outside influences.

"Ego has designed self denial well. There is very little room for any perspective or communication. But there is one saving grace — pain. When in self denial, you are systematically shutting down all the possible unlimited energy supplies and conversations with your Higher Self. Going in the completely opposite direction from your natural creative state, you feel pain. The resistance to feeling is what is actually being experienced. The more you deny your natural unlimited power, the more painful the experience becomes.

"The moment you break this self-imposed exile and choose to stop the pain, Higher Self is there shining light into the pit that you've been digging. How deep the pit is depends on how long you have been denying your own Heart and playing the victim."

"So last night I blew all my extra acceleration by going over the top?" I ventured.

"Well, you gained an accelerated insight that we are discussing now. But you did it the hard way," came the reply. "You're back in balance now. It's just that you have to go through a few painful adjustments to reacquaint yourself with your *normal*. Hence the energetic dehydration."

"I'd hardly call this, *normal*." I said, rolling my eyes into the back of my inner universe. "But that hyper state last night wasn't normal for here," I admitted.

"Well, it was normal for Ego. But if you'd carried on you would have become more and more isolated from Life and your Heart. Think of your awareness as a giant bubble gum bubble."

"Okay, when I experiment in my Life I can do it through Ego or Heart. If the intention behind my expansion is loving then my bubble will expand and keep on expanding because love is unending. If the motive is Ego driven then the bubble will soon burst and I'll be disconnected from RealLife, albeit temporarily," I ventured.

"Yes. Trying to expand with only Ego as your adviser means that the bubble bursts sooner rather than later. You are left hanging at the mercy of Ego, disconnected from your greater world until you can get back to your

Heart. Remember, you aren't doing anything wrong, you are simply discovering which paths create expansion and which paths are dead-ends created by Ego. It's all part of your research. Always go with the flow and remain open hearted and open-minded for this is the key. It is only when you deny your Heart or push joyous states to extreme imbalance that you will become disconnected from your guidance and your Life."

"So when the room started spinning, my bubble burst and I was disconnected from Life?"

"Yes. But you didn't come back completely empty-handed. You had your hangover! The reminder of your excursion into Ego."

"Well, now that you mention it, my headache is coming back." I began to rub my forehead.

"So, do you want to stay here?" asked my Higher Self changing the subject.

"I don't know," I paused. "Can I have a sleep and tell you later?"

"Of course. Call me when you get up. You know where I am."

"Yes I do," I said drowsily.

Ego under acceleration

Awaking after only an hour, the drill in my head was replaced with a refreshing calm and a return to honesty that confirmed I was in no state for another intensive tutorial. I felt like a day off. I wanted to sift through the download of realizations and wisdoms and get to grips with the tools I was supposed to be wielding. This was my idea of a steady recovery.

Going into town had no appeal, not because of the previous night's exploits but more because its beat offered no relaxation. If I were honest, I had changed, not the city. Now

I only required a short stay to get my fill of thrills. A part of me was horrified to admit I'd slowed down, couldn't take the pace anymore. But that wasn't it. I hadn't understood the pace, the contrast between masculine and feminine energy environments before. All I'd wanted was activity on fast forward. But for the first time, I'd stopped. I hadn't rushed back into what demanded my attention. My environment hadn't chosen me, I'd chosen it. City buzz was finally in context and I was looking further afield for my relaxation.

I could feel my Higher Self standing close to me as if we'd stopped conversing in mid sentence and I was yet to give my reply. I remembered my Higher Self's question.

"Well, I think I'd prefer to stay here at the moment. It's the acceleration that concerns me right now. Everything is becoming more demanding and the rate we are moving through these experiences is speeding up. Today I want to learn how to cope with processing; I'm a little blurred at the edges."

"Shall we go for a drive?" asked my Higher Self, changing the subject as if my request for a break had gone unnoticed. I was speechless.

"I was thinking of taking a break, giving myself a chance to be like a caterpillar: eat, sleep, dry out and transform."

My Higher Self carried on with the enticements. "You can travel at whatever speed you like. We don't have to rush anywhere. What do you feel? Blow away a few cobwebs? After all, you are feeling better, aren't you?"

"Alright, I surrender." Gesturing like an auctioneer — 'going once, going twice, going three times' — I confirmed the purchase with the falling of an imaginary hammer. "¬One spontaneous excursion sold to the person with the blue car."

Maneuvering slowly and deliberately out of the car park, I indicated right in the direction of the Eastern ring road, out of town. The fuel tank was looking a little low. "What shall we do about the petrol?" I asked my Higher Self.

"Just keep driving. There will be more than enough, you'll see."

"Where are we going?" I asked, not really expecting an answer.

"You don't need to know your destination to believe you are making progress," came the cryptic reply.

"Well, I suppose it's a comfort, though, to know where you are going. It gives you a target to aim for," I continued.

"So you find a limit comforting?" came the agile response.

I realized what I'd said. "Yes, I suppose I still do," I admitted, feeling caught out.

"That wasn't a trick," paused my Higher Self, "just an opportunity to be honest. Being honest with yourself is one of the most effective ways to get you back in the flow, beyond any limits. At the moment, you are most likely to accelerate because you don't know where you are going; you have no limits on your direction or capability. Are you going to drive quickly or slowly now that you don't know your final destination?" challenged my Higher Self.

"There is no inclination to do either so I'll drive how I feel; keep balanced and go with the flow I suppose."

"You'll go with the flow?"

"Yes, I suppose so. Yes," I reaffirmed.

"Then, if you keep balanced, maximum acceleration is yours," came the guidance.

"Talking of balance, I meant to ask you before I fell asleep… when I was out on the town disempowering myself, why didn't you come to my aid? You could have changed your wavelength, tuned in on my level."

"To what end?" came the response.

"Because you are my Higher Self, and you are here to support me in the journey to RealLife," I replied with a measure of disappointment.

"Yes, that is part of the service."

"So why did you let me down?" I moaned.

"It isn't possible for anyone but you to let yourself down in the sense of disempowerment," replied my Higher Self promptly. "It may appear strange now, but you chose to lower your vibration just as you choose everything else on this journey of discovery. If you had been rescued, it would have hindered you greatly. It would have been a disservice that your Ego could use to its advantage. No one can live your Life for you, nor can they do your learning for you. Without the practical you can't gain wisdom."

I got a glimpse of my victimhood. It didn't look pretty. My Higher Self seemed to nod gently in recognition.

"So if you'd helped me, you would have been rescuing me from myself... or in other words, controlling me!" I acknowledged.

"Precisely. Intervention would have been anything but Divine! Such interference would have been robbing you of the very realizations you are now consciously embracing. Unconditional Love is the allowance of ignorance as much as it is the celebration of learning. Both are capable of engendering wisdom."

A sudden wave of tiredness began to overwhelm me. "I want a break," I said forcefully.

"As you wish." My Higher Self fell silent.

The countryside was now covered in a dense collage of tea bushes, all unique pieces in Nature's private jigsaw puzzle. The land fell away abruptly as the plantations ended and the road descended sharply towards a lake. I could see a few walking tracks disappearing into clusters of giant bamboo, mahogany and blue gum trees. I was now feeling incredibly tired and anxiously looking for a place to get off the road. Much to my relief, there was a picnic area around the next bend. I parked the car and let out a sigh of fatigue.

Although I was incredibly tired, I couldn't relax. Sitting in the car felt claustrophobic so I opened the door to let in some fresh air. My next breath was filled with an intense burst of fresh sunshine and pine. Mustering up all my energy, I left the car in search of a patch of grass where I could stretch out and relax. As the trees thinned I could see a large lake. Its shoreline was dotted with houseboats and pontoons. My surge of energy had all but dissipated and I was now in desperate need of a place to lie down. The intermittent rocks and carpet of pine needles were less than inviting but a boat jetty stretched out before me, dry and warm in the afternoon sun. I lay down on the warm planks and fell into a deep sleep.

Suddenly, I heard a shout; someone calling me. I woke with a start. It was an old man in a small wooden rowing boat waving to attract my attention.

"Come on, queue up please," he shouted. As the feisty little boat nudged its way through the water with each tenacious stroke of the oars, I began to see the man's features more clearly. He had a welcoming, swarthy face with a shock of ill-kempt hair and a gaze that would melt the iciest of rebukes.

"Time to fish," he said cheerfully as he brought the boat alongside.

"Permission to dock?" he requested formally.

"Permission granted," I replied, struggling to my feet.

"Well, I'm only stopping to pick up passengers," he said warily, "so don't go charging me a landing fee."

"I wouldn't do that," I said, almost offended.

"Good. Always important to check the lie of the land," he replied with comic efficiency.

"No lying here," I grinned, standing back to make way for his passengers.

I was just about to turn around and see who was behind me when the old man asked impatiently, "Well, are you coming fishing or not?"

"Who, me?" I looked over both shoulders, checking for passengers.

"Do you see any other me's here?" he said quizzically.

"No." I paused, trying to formulate a polite rejection. "But to be honest, I don't really like fishing. Too much patience and smelly bait for my liking."

"That's all right. I was really only offering you a lift. The fishing is optional, a kind of means to an end."

"Sounds intriguing." I stepped into the boat and sat opposite my newfound ferryman. The boat surged skillfully forward as we headed for the other side of the lake. When we were half way across, the ferryman pulled in the oars declaring, "Let me introduce myself, I'm your friendly pirate and as I'm going to rob you, I'd like to know your name first."

I felt myself jolt backwards, then I stopped. "You're joking right?" I ventured.

"Of course, I am. But it's obviously not working because you're not laughing yet! I'll try another one: What lies at the bottom of the sea and quivers?"

"I don't know. What lies at the bottom of the sea and quivers?"

"A nervous wreck!"

This time I laughed without any cue and, as though a laughter pipeline had opened up somewhere high in the clouds, we showered in gurgles of giggles until the clouds dissolved and our channel was no more.

"Well, tell me, my friendly pirate; ever considered being a stand up comic?"

"What? In this boat? The audience would be sea sick in no time!" he laughed.

"No, seriously. You're a great story teller."

"Well, actually I am an entertainer. I'm a type of magician—a fizz-ician!"

"Do you mean physician? What area of medicine?"

"Oh, general health and well being. What about you? What's your occupation?"

"I'm a professional traveler."

"How long have you been going?"

"Well..." I paused, puzzled at a question about linear time. It seemed so long since I'd considered time, let alone had anyway to measure it. "I've lost track of time. It's an elusive quantity these days. If I were honest, I can't really remember when I started. I suppose it's been quite a while."

"Is that why you were so tired back there?" he continued.

"Sort of. It's been pretty intense of late." I paused self consciously, knowing that if I continued I was likely to dampen the frivolity.

"Go on... I'm intrigued." It was as if my companion had been reading my thoughts.

"Well, I've been thinking about everything that I am required to do, and the more I understand, the more there seems to be to discover. Don't get me wrong, I'm not trying to know it all; I'm well beyond that. It's just that each greater insight leads to another greater learning and then a greater insight. Sometimes it's like going nowhere. I don't know whether to congratulate myself on how far I've come or be downhearted because there is still so far to go."

"If I were you, I'd get over your resistance to both of them first, then you'll know what you really feel. No point in bottling yourself up between the devil and the deep blue sea," he smiled reassuringly. "Appreciate your effort in the moment."

My blank expression showed my lack of understanding. The friendly pirate stretched his legs out as if he was showing me.

"You see, it's like this," he said. "Joy isn't something you can cramp into a corner. If you suppress your joy then you'll be like someone who jumps into this lake, diving through their fears to discover buried treasure. And then, when they've found it, they still persist in swimming through the sediment rather than bringing their find to the surface and appreciating it. The pirate in me says 'Treasure your find, however small or great, and re-invest it wisely.' Life's to be taken seriously, not solemnly."

There was a long pause.

"Well, my dear traveler," continued the pirate-cum-ferryman, "I will give you much more than a penny for your thoughts. In fact, they've been so valuable that they've more than paid for this trip. I believe if you look behind, you will see the conclusion to this part of your journey."

Suddenly, I felt my face wet with something. I opened my eyes to see a large friendly mongrel sharing his wet coat with me and licking my face. I bumped noses with the boisterous dog as I sat up from where I was lying. He took that as a playful challenge and started barking at me as if I was holding an imaginary stick. His owner called breathlessly as she puffed behind, hurrying to restrain her charge.

"That's Oliver, friend to one and all," she spluttered apologetically.

"Well, his affectionate manner keeps you fit," I joked.

"You never said a truer word. But he makes up in charm what he lacks in obedience."

"Great trade off," I agreed, smiling.

"Warm today," said the dog walker, finally getting her breath back. "Have you been sleeping long?"

"I have no idea," I said, taken aback by her question.

"Well, come on Oliver, it's dinner time."

"Just before you go… did you see the man in the boat?" I ventured hurriedly.

"What man in a boat?" she said, confused at my question.

"He dropped me off just a minute ago," I added.

"Oh, I didn't see any boat, just you lying on the jetty. Sorry I can't help you." She turned away towards the dog.

"Come on Oliver. Now, where did I put your lead?" she said absent mindedly, looking in her pockets while hurrying after Oliver as he sped towards the trees like a people-seeking missile.

I felt refreshed and strangely energized leaving the lake. For a day of doing nothing, it had been truly fulfilling.

"Doing nothing?" echoed my Higher Self.

"Well, not exactly nothing. More a case of allowing being," I acknowledged.

"Indeed. Today you beat your Ego at its own game," said my Higher Self.

"That being?" I asked, hoping for an incoming achievement.

"You started to look into yourself; a bit of self reflection. Looking at yourself used to be something you did in the mirror, a vanity that reinforced the superficiality of your fragile Ego image. Now when you look into whatever 'mirror' you have chosen, you see more of how you can unlimit yourself with response rather than reaction. Bravo! Take a bow!"

I took a bow in all directions, acknowledging the applause of my imaginary audience and the departing sun as it sank in the west.

"Ego has been with you for the duration of your Limitation. All its best resistance clones such as avoidance, apathy and doubt are manufactured from observing the 'limited you'. Reactions such as anger, disappointment and blame are all created from Ego's demand to stop the flow of creation. Today you moved through one of your biggest blocks yet, and it wasn't related to how hard you worked. Your day wasn't arduous was it?"

"If I said yes, I'd be lying. It took a lot of surrender and a bit of flexibility but once I got on a roll it was simple. It was much easier than finding a hotel," I acknowledged.

"Well, when Ego is in control, it can siphon off most of your creation fuel into resistance and conflict. Ego can exhaust you by encouraging you to energize your resistance over and over again. But now you have the tools of self observation and self enquiry to help you recognize the Ego's antics within yourself and your environment. Next time you meet Ego, not only will you be able to say no, you will be able to flow through the meeting and out the other side without any major imbalance. So, welcome to your ease and increased flow," announced my Higher Self. "Today you didn't give Ego a chance to keep you limited, you came out and faced it. Your relentless commitment to self understanding sent your Ego running into its remaining darkness."

"Thank you. I couldn't have done it without you."

"No you couldn't simply because we are never separate."

"Well, what I mean to say is that I really appreciate your help with getting this far. I was beginning to flake a bit but now everything feels worthwhile."

We sat in a twilight friendship that seemed to extend out in all directions until the moist evening air brought the desire to return to the car.

"Shall we walk back?" I asked my Higher Self.

"What about a walk along the lake front before you retire for the evening?"

"Done."

A full moon was visible in the early evening sky and the lake now had a magical silver sheen rippling gently towards shore. The sky was devoid of clouds but studded with diamond constellations sparkling just out of reach. As I walked I could see a small converted houseboat only a few hundred meters in the distance. An outside light cast gold into the silver of the moonlight. "I wonder if this is where the friendly pirate lives," I said, half rhetorically, half hoping my Higher Self would enlighten me with the answer. But there was no reply; my Higher Self appeared to have retired for the evening.

The modest but welcoming dwelling was called the Travelers Rest. I decided to knock on the door and satisfy my curiosity. Instead, it opened before I could turn the handle. All was wood and the smell of linseed oil. The lounge opened into a bedroom that had double doors opening onto a small balcony. The large glass doors framed the lake view perfectly, just as if you were sitting in front of a painting.

I returned to the lounge and saw a note pad propped against a jar of coffee. It read: 'Poetry is like peace; it can be interpreted in many different ways but it is rarely embraced completely. Bless this house with your peace of Mind, Body and Spirit and you will spread its significance throughout your travels. Be welcomed.'

The beauty of the words was all the invitation I required to embrace this perfect flow of hospitality. As I curled up between the rich cotton sheets, I surrendered to the embrace of the full moon and a night full of the poetry of peace.

Home is where the Heart is

The next morning I awoke with a curious feeling of anticipation. This was going to be a great day, but I had no idea why.

"Good Morning Higher Self. Are you up yet?" I teased.

"You rang?" came the reply with a butler's lilt.

"Do you ever get the feeling that something wonderful is about to happen?"

"All the time," smiled my Higher Self.

"But you just don't know what it's going to be," I hinted, hoping my Higher Self would enlighten me.

"Does it have to be just one thing?" was the reply, ignoring my hint.

"I suppose not. But something fundamental has changed, of that I am sure. I just don't know what exactly," I rambled.

"Well, if that'll be all, I'll leave you to your discovery."

"I don't suppose you can tell me what this significant something is?"

My Higher Self was silent.

"I'll take that as a no," I said, sitting up in bed and looking through the balcony doors into a new canvas of the lake. It was now a beautiful Prussian blue rippling intermittently as breezes chased each other across its surface. 'So what is different?' I asked myself, returning to my search. 'How have I changed?' An image of the car accelerated across my mind. 'I'm going to get a new car?' I could feel my Higher Self wince. 'Okay, it's not that. So I've just undergone a type of acceleration that has created a different feel to my world.' I could feel my Higher Self encouraging me like we were playing cosmic charades.

'So now I'm traveling and driving differently. Before I had a destination and I drove to it. But now I'm really letting go. I'm not letting the destination dictate my level of fulfillment. I'm also not driving with only the destination in mind. I'm expressing my intentions while letting the Universe show me how they can come into being. This is being in command without being in control. What is experienced is always my choice, it's just that I'm now cooperating on a deeper level with the Universe.'

I fell back on the pillows under the weight of realization.

"This is heavy stuff!" I feigned exhaustion.

My Higher Self was unimpressed. "Carry on. You haven't finished yet," came the observation.

I groaned and sat up again. But my Higher Self hadn't finished.

"To continue, perhaps the biggest part of this shift is that I don't feel driven anymore. I want to be in RealLife but I'm not putting myself under pressure to get there. There is no rush, only learning. All I require is in front of me in each moment. All that's required of me is to be flexible; vary my rate of processing so I don't accelerate too fast and miss any helpful insights or discoveries. Today I'm really feeling what it's like to go with the flow. Before, I wanted to do it but not be it. Now, I'm sufficiently allowing to experience the result of my choices, not just think I have experienced it. No more trying to make it happen, I am choosing and then co-creating with the Universe. No force, just flow."

I showered and dressed quickly and then perched at the end of my bed as if awaiting instructions.

"So what are you waiting for?" asked my Higher Self.

"Nothing. Except perhaps clarifying my intentions for today!"

"Those being…?"

"I am creating and embracing the flow and experience of RealLife in all its forms."

"Wonderful. And without further ado, let RealLife commence!" announced my Higher Self.

I left my room and unlocked the car. I was finally in the driver's seat of my Life. I started the engine and moved onto the road. I Looked at the petrol gauge, there was a full tank. I felt a surge of fulfillment, slowing down had been exactly what was required to get all my learning into context and appreciate how far I'd come. There was no point in making progress if I didn't know I'd done it. That's why my Higher Self had told me not to worry—everything was going to filter through and I'd have the fuel I needed. A feeling of pure connectedness filled every cell of my body; no resistance, no polarity, no barriers.

As I drove, every aspect of my vision looked just that little bit greener, brighter, and larger than life, and yet surrounded by more space. The road remained a single lane in each direction and even though there was considerably more traffic, all was flowing within a chaotic perfection. I didn't wonder where all the extra vehicles had come from, nor did I try to compete or avoid them. I just drove.

Junction fourteen was fast approaching and there was a

sign reading 'Amusement Park'. I felt a rush through my body so I indicated and turned off in the direction of the sign.

The park was full of everything that would have been considered out-of-this-world in Existence, but which now appeared totally normal. It was a non-stop flow of joy inviting you to join the ride of your Life.

"Is RealLife an endless flow of purpose?" I queried.

"In a way, yes. There is certainly no waste or lack in RealLife because there is no limitation," answered my Higher Self.

"How come it took me so long to work this part out?" I continued.

"Well, for one thing, you had linear time," joked my Higher Self.

"Ego?"

"Indeed. And that was the reason for your research."

"So when I was in the depths of Existence there was no way this degree of flow, detachment and allowance could have been recognized?"

"Precisely. The structure in Existence is simply too dense to accommodate it. There is only room for Ego. When you were in Existence you sought to densify your experience by concentrating it with more and more doing. You were literally missing in action because you did one action after another with no purpose, day in and day out. This created less and less space for expansion and more and more Ego control. Now the reverse is occurring. It's just taken you until this moment to appreciate just how much space you have made within yourself, for yourself."

"So now, the more choice I have, the more space I can create and the more opportunities I have to embrace Life and RealLife."

"Yes. This is part of the fulfillment… or perhaps it would be better to call it re-fillment! You are, after all, re-filling your life with balance and purpose."

"So now I am no longer creating with half my resources?"

"Go on..." prompted my Higher Self.

"Well, instead of doing without purpose, now I'm doing and being with purpose, striking a balance between detachment, action, intuition and allowance."

"Indeed. Carry on..."

"Doing without choice or without understanding my intention becomes 'trying.' This is what the Existors are doing — trying. And that's why their experience is such a struggle — they aren't refilling or becoming fulfilled, they are continually concentrating their imbalance."

"Exactly. So if you want to continually empower your fulfillment, what are you going to choose?"

"Unify action and intention, go with the flow and use the tools I have at my disposal in a balanced way."

"So what are you waiting for?" asked my Higher Self jokingly.

"You to finish your sentence," I replied cheekily.

I left the car and entered the amusement park. I screamed and laughed my way through ride after ride until it was time to take on fuel in the form of lunch.

"What's on the menu?" I gasped. "I can't eat air any more!"

"What kind of nourishment would you like?" enquired my Higher Self.

"Well, something simple, fresh, tasty," I replied eagerly.

"I know just the place. Follow me..." came the reply.

My hunger focused my efforts and I was back in the car quicker than I could have imagined or understood. Instead of rejoining the motorway, we carried on parallel and stopped at a café close to a farm shop selling locally grown produce and handicrafts.

By now I was ravenous and everything I saw looked appetizing. I decided to choose my lunch from the color combinations on display. I feasted on verdant green, rich magenta and vibrant orange. Looking past all the café chairs and tables, I could see more bursts of bright red and green. Beyond the courtyard was a canal with clusters of houseboats moored together in huddles of three, as if gossiping about their owners or onlookers gazing coyly from the bank.

I walked down towards the canal to admire the intricate decorative patterns on each boat. Some were like floating gardens, full to bursting with potted plants and window boxes. One even had its own putting green. A head of auburn curls popped up from inside a boat named Bertha.

"What an unusual house you have," I remarked.

"Yes. Not exactly what springs to mind for most people, but it's more of a home than any I've had on dry land."

"Permission to come aboard," I requested.

"Permission granted. Do you want a cup of something? I'm just putting the kettle on," the friendly voice continued as she descended below.

"That would be great," I agreed.

"Mind your head…" But I hit my head on the front door as I negotiated my way to the lounge and dining room.

"Oh, sorry. Too late! Are you all right?"

"Yeah, it didn't hurt," I replied, rubbing my head. "Looks like there's no pain in all this careful workmanship, only TLC."

"Thank you. I'll take that as a compliment," replied the owner while burying her head in one of the kitchen cupboards. "What brought you here? Most people don't get as far as this unless they have an interest in the handicrafts," she added candidly.

"Well, I was just wandering actually. I went to the Amusement Park and kept on going. I'm a spontaneous tourist today."

"The best way to be. Any beautiful postcards along the way?" enquired my host.

"I don't have a conventional camera but there are plenty of snapshots stored in my Heart. Less weight. I'm becoming more and more conscious about possessions. Don't want to fill up the important areas of my life with 'things'; had my fill of that. Still, I expect you know that only too well, living on a houseboat."

"Yes, I threw out a lot of physical memories when I came to float here. Still, when I was at the point of letting go, it wasn't that difficult; more a part of a natural cycle rather than a big wrench. It's amazing how you can do a lot more with what appears to be less," she confirmed.

"I hadn't thought of it like that." I paused.

She continued. "It's a bit like being able to see the wood as well as the trees! It's as if you have cosmic bifocals — you can see your vision as well as the details straight in front of you, all in one combined prospect. All you are required to do is choose which part of the lens to look through and filter your life accordingly. Quite an achievement, living in the flow."

"Do you like living on something that is always moving, never having anything truly solid in your life?" I was curious.

"Well, I can't really say a time, event or moment when I stopped feeling the bobbing motion of the boat, but I certainly wouldn't choose to go back to living without that feeling. It's as if I've traded in solidity for fluidity or, to put it another way, exchanged rigidity for flexibility. No longer am I content to move about a fixed point; I've chosen to join a bigger cycle that connects with my old ways but lets me release them gracefully. Similar to an abode that is always rebuilding itself, the boat never feels the same from one day to the next. It's the ultimate: a new house every day."

We talked for hours about discovering what was truly fulfilling and empowering, and about days like the one I was experiencing, days when everything flowed seamlessly. Cups of tea turned into light snacks and then the daylight began to fade. The conversation came full circle and I rose to leave.

"Thanks for all your insights and hospitality." I paused. "One last question... Don't I know you from somewhere? I know it sounds corny but I really feel like I've been here before. Not so much the boat but the sensation of having been in your company at another time. Have we met?"

"Yes and no. You haven't met me in my current form, although we are definitely on the same wavelength, as it were. I know who you have been and where you are now. Tomorrow however, you won't recognize me, nor will you return to this place. Your acceleration is such that this space and these experiences will no longer be relevant to your perception. You'll be looking into the next aspect of your world. This doesn't diminish the empowerment of our exchanges, just puts them into your ever expanding perspective. But that's the nature of the service these meetings provide; there is so much to be gained but there's no point in getting attached. There's no scarcity in RealLife; nothing to lose or miss out on."

She smiled before completing her summary. "What's important is that you recognize when you are in a vibration that unifies your inner and outer worlds. Our conversation has been constructed of such moments; a constant flow of harmony and abundant ease; both a subtle expansion and a delicate inducement to continue on your journey, to meet others like yourself and more of RealLife's nature. It's been a real pleasure. Let me give you this small token of my appreciation."

I smiled broadly as my host pressed what appeared to be a small figure on a key ring into my hand, then vanished below deck. As I opened my hand to look more closely, I saw an Eagle, with outstretched wings. On his chest was written 'Trust your Heart' and across his wings 'Minds are like wings; they only function when open'.

I am present

As I walked back from the canal past the now-closed café, I realized just how tempting it was to try and keep hold of this feeling; to fear the loss of RealLife instead of believing that it was always an option, ready to be chosen. I wanted this to go on forever and was tempted to suggest it to my Higher Self.

"Today has been truly wonderful. I'd love it to go on forever," I hinted heavily, waiting for my Higher Self to fill in how this could be achieved.

"Limiting your fulfillment options again, eh?" came the reply.

"I'd like to think of it more as maintaining my level of fulfillment," I said apologetically.

"You won't achieve that by becoming attached and limiting the flow."

"No, you're right, as usual. If I tried to maintain the same level of fulfillment, I'd end up just like my Ego, controlling my world and stopping the unlimited flow. Scarcity is such a strong conditioning… Of course there's plenty more experiences to be created in RealLife. All I'm required to do is believe it into reality. Dreams can be my everyday reality." I paused. "Another question about today… I can't help feeling that the lady on the houseboat sounded exactly like you…" I lingered mid-sentence.

"That's because it was me. Well… us," replied my Higher Self gently. "Remember, RealLife is true home and there is no limit to the form or expression of those residing in RealLife. When all is in harmony it can flow effortlessly while maintaining purpose. Yes, you've met before… we've met before… whichever way you look at it. We will continue to meet: different boats, different purpose, but always navigating to your next port of call… or ours, depending on your perspective."

"So why don't you just talk to me in my Heart, the direct route as it were?" I was puzzled at this apparent inefficiency.

"Sometimes it is important to demonstrate to yourself the degree of harmony and rebalancing you have achieved. As a result your Heart spills into your surroundings. You meet what you are. You've experienced the Ego version of this."

"The hitchhiker?" I interjected.

"Yes indeed. So now it's time for reflections of a higher nature. These remind you that you are not separate from the world you create and everything is unified in the Grand Flow. This is all part of RealLife."

We were both silent but I could still feel the connectedness between us.

"So if an aspect of you appears from time to time here in this reality, where do you live the rest of the time?" I was suddenly enlivened by my new line of enquiry.

"In your Heart. My headquarters is the IAM Center — Inner Authority Mentor Center."

"So you're actually renting from me?"

"Well, we're both renting from the Universe actually." replied my Higher Self, having anticipated my question, "but we don't have a landlord as such. Rather, we've given ourselves the space to occupy, and the more change we can accommodate, the greater its capacity."

"So IAM is where RealLife expands from. The more balanced, aware and conscious we are in our intentions and creations, the more the IAM expands and the more RealLife we experience. IAM both orchestrates and consolidates our changes. You used to be cooped up because the IAM Center wasn't used and so there wasn't much space."

"Yes, that's correct. There wasn't much to work with because you weren't choosing, you were Existing. Then you came here and you accelerated your options. Now we've moved in together because you are choosing consciously and are less under the influence of Ego."

"So it's the reverse for Ego then?"

"In simple terms, yes. The mind is Ego's headquarters and the more unlimited thoughts you have, the less partitions and divisions there can be in your mind. So Ego is now existing in the areas of your mind that are most densely built up with your remaining conditioning and, yes, this means Ego has less choice about the limits it can impose upon you."

"Ego's got less choice about limitation. That's a good one!"

"Yes, quite an irony," replied my Higher Self.

"So Ego is lurking in the dimly lit corridors of my conditioned mind waiting to trip me up?" I surmised.

"Fight for your limitations and they are yours! Believe you can walk freely because you choose to, and it will be so," came the reality check.

"Don't put into words what you don't want?" I suggested apologetically.

"More importantly, don't even put intentions into what you don't want," replied my Higher Self.

"So, no room for victims in the house of IAM."

"None. The door is never locked but it can only be opened with the key of Choice. If you choose to go to your IAM then you are always welcome. Staying requires that you are disciplined about your thoughts, words and actions."

"So the longer I spend in IAM, the more choices I will relate to?"

"Absolutely. Creating within IAM on a regular basis becomes an abundant joy instead of a hit-and-miss struggle. The more thoughts you nourish within IAM, the more you will create what you want." My Higher Self fell quiet.

"This is really energizing. What other hints can you give me to make IAM my permanent home… and RealLife a permanent experience?"

"Well, after acclimatizing to the self disciplines of IAM, your consciousness will expand to a level at which all thoughts flow through the IAM. Love will be the strength within you that harmonizes all conflict, control and separation within your world. Your Heart will be permanently open and you will reside continually within your IAM. Limited creation will then dissolve into a permanent flow of instantaneous and constant creation. You will be actually living the dream. More importantly, you will have returned to RealLife—your Higher and Lower agendas will have merged. You will be reunified."

I felt simultaneously exhausted, elated and speechless. Everything had come together in one short statement. It was as if I'd been looking through a camera with only a close up lens, but now I had a wide angle view.

I searched for words to match my thoughts. "Well, it's great to know I have my own personal interface with the rest of the Universe."

"Yes. And you now have a place to be when the reflections of Limitation are dissolving around you. IAM will be your continuity while the outside world reconfigures to reflect the changes you are undergoing… Do you want a break?"

"No, I'm not quite saturated yet. Please continue," I replied.

"Think of IAM as an open house for the wise of the cosmos. You can discuss all your responses and experiences and how best to use the tools at your disposal. I am always here but in RealLife you aren't limited to one cosmic teacher. There are many others you can meet with; all you are required to do is invite the change while you are in IAM."

"Great—a cosmic get-together," I confirmed.

"Indeed. But before you go inviting everyone remember, IAM is your consolidation space and will expand most readily when you yourself are balanced. The other Masters in Light will always encourage you to change but even in IAM, you will sometimes think you have more capacity to change than you really have. And when you reject the self discipline and responsibilities that it takes to maintain your IAM, then it will take longer to rebuild your ability than you think. So appreciate what you are building. IAM consolidates all your Enerjewels and your tools, and it gives you all round vision."

"So does that mean I can have eyes in the back on my head?" I joked, but my Higher Self didn't register my flippancy.

"No, just an unending vision in all directions."

There was a long silence. And I knew better than to disturb the peace.

"You're learning. Well done. Balance is indeed what opens the door. Welcome home," I heard my Higher Self say as if savoring the phrase.

I felt an indescribable wave of love and peace. I could feel parts of my being I had never known before. Sensation flowed into a picture; I was looking around a room within my Heart home. It was a bit dusty but it had a purposeful air, as if it was ready to be filled with the furniture of unlimited thought and decorated with loving intention.

"So what do you feel?" my Higher Self asked me.

"It could do with some work," I observed. "But that's what the IAM is all about, right? Conscious efforts?"

"Indeed. And with no denial, struggle or attachment you'll be creating instantaneously in no time at all."

"Yes, in no time at all," I said. "Because this is what being self employed is all about," I added.

"Exactly! This is where a true Life's work starts," agreed my Higher Self.

Now time

The next day I was determined to continue with my spontaneous tourism and I assumed that my Higher Self was in agreement. I didn't bother asking where we were going because it wasn't necessary. I just wanted to eliminate the need to 'do'; surrender completely to the flow and feel the liberation and expansion of my consolidating connection. Yesterday I had started the process but today I would achieve being within it fully. But first some food.

I headed straight to the hotel restaurant to fill up with fuel for the day's excursion. The waitress gave me a menu; I placed my order without glancing through it.

"Coffee and an omelet, please. And could you make that soonish — I'm eager to get on the road."

"Fine. We're a bit busy today but I'll do my best," replied the waitress.

"Thanks, I really appreciate it," I said, trying to smile my omelet into being. I sat enjoying the tantalizing aromas of coffee and toast.

What appeared to be an age went by and the coffee still hadn't arrived.

"You've got plenty of time, you know," observed my Higher Self.

"But I'm eager to get on the road," I insisted.

"Why?"

"Because we're going exploring again."

"Are we?"

"What do you mean?" I asked pointedly, feeling my plans and expectations falling apart.

"Traveling by car isn't in the flow at present. But we will still be in maximum acceleration right here. Do you want to stay here?"

I felt anger beginning to rise within me.

"I've got better things to do than sit in a coffee shop all day," I exclaimed. "What's the point of that?" I paused in the middle of a rising justification. I floated outside of my physical body and saw Ego on my face, angrily squeezing itself into my words, fighting for, and even defending, the very limitation I thought I was dissolving. I fell silent. I'd recognized my resistance and I knew I'd fallen through the thin walls of my IAM and was heading straight into the arms of Ego.

"Sorry," I said disappointedly. "I was arguing with you though you are trying to help me."

"You aren't required to apologize," responded my Higher Self, "you've done nothing wrong. But just remember, it takes two to argue so conflict between us is impossible. You were arguing with Ego, who was impersonating the higher aspects. And now that you're challenging Ego at greater and greater depths, it's changing strategy. Until recently, simple fear was enough to keep you limited. But now you've found your IAM Center, Ego has given up direct and obvious confrontations in favor of more subtle disturbances.

"Since yesterday Ego has been carefully encouraging you to become attached to your past instead of responding to the flow of learning that is right in front of you. Living in the past caused you to start arguing with your present. You began dissipating your energy in anger when your expectations weren't met. It's similar to pelting yourself with rotten tomatoes but perhaps a little less messy! Fortunately the energetic brawl stopped after the first few missiles because you realized you were arguing with yourself."

"So this was an opportunity to watch my Ego at work?" I observed soberly.

"Yes. And choosing to stop conflict has given you the acceleration you were looking for earlier, albeit in a different way. Before you reacted for longer periods, giving your Ego more and more fuel. But now you're no longer bouncing, reacting and ricocheting off your life experience. Instead you are beginning to flow through it. Less of the Pinball Wizard, more of the Wizard."

"So if I want to get the most out of the flow of experience then when I meet these Ego episodes, it's to be the least reactive that I can. And if I remain in my IAM Center then I will be able to convert the resistance into expansion; allow the game to unfold while I focus on expanding my IAM Center rather than fighting with my Ego. The more capable I become at staying centered, the more fuel I will recycle and the greater my acceleration."

"You've got it. The less you rebound off your Life and the more you change your perspective and go through Ego, the more you are going to expand until the acceleration doesn't bother you any more. Ego becomes amusing, not upsetting, as you marvel at the ways it tries to stop you embracing your natural creativity. You are now beginning to believe and see that you are an Unlimited Creator. Gone are the days when Ego told you to 'get back in your box'!"

"So, don't fight; just change your mind?"

"Exactly. An unwavering commitment to understanding creates the flow, and Ego friction becomes reduced to a minimum. One change of belief after another; one acceleration after another."

"But I thought miracles were reserved for the risen, not for a soul seeker at my level," I questioned, as if trying to find a gap in this seamless wisdom.

"How do you think the risen became risen? It's a miracle you're here now!" laughed my Higher Self. "Part of the greater miracle is that you've stopped racing into an empty future and let your Higher Nature get a word in edgeways. Now you're awake, don't diminish your sense of achievement just because you didn't know exactly when you arrived in it. It's one unending achievement. Surprising yourself with your abilities will become a joy instead of something you dread because you have to brace yourself or try and avoid it. Nourish the miracle worker, the wizard, the magician in you," exclaimed my Higher Self excitedly.

"Wonderful," I affirmed. "I am the Pinball Wizard I seek to be."

"Of course. You are all that you seek," continued my Higher Self, "you are simply changing the way that you perceive it and express it. You were all that you seek when you were compressed into Limitation. You are still all that you seek, just seeking a different 'all' than you were."

"So the drive's cancelled?"

"Well from one point of view it appears that way. But if you are looking through the eyes of surrender, then nothing has been cancelled. All is in the flow."

"So, I am accelerating with the flow right here, right now," I smiled, putting on a brave face where disappointment had been.

"That is our never ending higher-way. Sometimes we go to the mountain, other times we bring the mountain to us. Either way, the view is beautiful if you can just focus through the Heart. Think of this leg of the journey as an inner expansion rather than an outer projection. It's part of settling into your chosen home — IAM Center. Wasn't that your commitment?"

I agreed that it was.

The waitress jogged my arm. "Sorry to interrupt your daydream but your food's here and you said you were in a hurry," she frowned.

"Thanks. I really appreciate the fast service but perhaps I'll be staying longer than I thought."

Her face dropped as if disappointed that she wasn't going to see the back of her demanding and indecisive customer sooner.

"Okay, as you wish," she sighed.

I felt a twinge of guilt.

"Now, why am I feeling like this?" I was compelled to ask. "I've made the right decision, haven't I?"

My Higher Self ignored my attempt at approval. "Whose expectations weren't met this time?" the tutorial continued.

"Well, mine of course… and the waitress's?" I ventured.

"Exactly. You cancelled her expectations without prior notice. Not easy for any Ego to handle."

"Carry on," I said to my Higher Self. "I'll eat, you talk." I tucked into my omelet.

"Guilt is a device that the Ego has been using ever since you arrived in Limitation. It's often the partner of unrequited expectation. When the ever-expanding world goes in a direction that you didn't expect, then guilt is Ego's result, instead of the realization that an expanding world can't be controlled by reactions and regrets.

"Guilt is one of the ways your Ego can keep you attached. It can happen through a wide range of circumstances. It's easy to feel guilty when you criticize or blame. Either way, 'your fault' becomes your drain. You feel weak and scattered whether you've just shouted at the guilty party or feel that you should be guilty for not meeting another's expectations."

I stopped eating as if to talk to my Higher Self. "So Ego is telling me that my change of plan has let the waitress down when all I've actually done is something I didn't expect. And from her perspective, I have done something she didn't expect. So it's just more uncertainty—an expansion that could be seen as resourceful and very efficient… But the waitress doesn't know about our discussion so for her, this uncertainty has no benefit. All she can see is that I'm sitting on my own and taking up a table that perhaps she would have filled twice by now… in her expectations, of course."

"So are you guilty?" asked my Higher Self.

"Well the only crime I'm guilty of is change; going with the flow!" I confirmed.

"Indeed. At moments like this, you can either do the Ego's work for it by reverting back to old conditioning… or you can choose differently."

"Going back to Limitation is just like going backwards. So instead of seeking refuge in the past, if I want to move forward then I am required to stay in the Now."

"Exactly. And where is the easiest place to do that?" asked my Higher Self.

"In my IAM. I'm not going to progress by hanging on to past memories of my fulfillment. Each moment is a unique opportunity to move forward, so there's no point in looking back to what was joyous when I have the opportunity to create it, and more, now."

"So I'll ask the question again. Do you want to leave the coffee shop?" said my Higher Self with a clarifying intensity.

"No. IAM here, now. I'm traveling wherever this takes me. I understand that I got temporarily ambushed by my own expectations, but being here doesn't mean I lose out. And I'm living in the past if I'm trying to create the same level of joy, in the same way as yesterday," I acknowledged. "It was Ego that was standing in my way, trying to convince me that I couldn't learn here and now. So now I understand I am choosing to stay here with you and continue my learning. Just because I don't like it doesn't mean it isn't of service to me." Now I felt comfortable.

"Indeed." My Higher Self paused. "Perhaps at these times the best way to deal with Ego is to consider it as a spoilt child. Once upon a time you gave this child control but it wasn't enough. You gave it more because of your commitment to your research in Limitation. Then, you gave it still more control and began building a monster fuelled by your constant concessions. Now the child is an adult, it's learnt all its tricks from observing your reactions so it can react to almost any challenge you give it. That is, all except one—detachment. When you are detached you are in your IAM and can see through Ego distractions."

"But people often refer to detachment as being unfeeling, uncaring, even selfish," I contested.

"That's how Ego refers to detachment because it doesn't want anyone to use this valuable tool. Detachment is like a knife. It cuts through Ego ties and brings you clarity. When you utilize detachment, you can appreciate what is the central foundation of your experience—Fear or Love. Detachment unravels the complicated knots of Ego. When you detach, you love yourself enough to stop fear and you change your mind to embrace genuine Love. Detachment always creates alternatives. Alternatives are choice and choice is love."

"So if I'm detached then I don't stop loving, just stop giving Ego attention? And I look at my experience more objectively, with more clarity?"

"Yes. Many may accuse you of not caring but really it's their Ego saying 'You don't care about me any more.' You know that if you care about them truly, you will support them in alternatives, not in more escalating dramas, complications and struggles."

"So the next time the Cosmic Brat tries it on, I'll laugh with him, not at him. And no matter how much Ego dramatizes, coerces and prods me, I won't react and I won't take on board its attempts to convince me that my alternatives won't work!"

"Wonderful… Finished eating? Or do you still have an appetite for learning?" queried my Higher Self.

"Well, I'm quite full but I'm sure I could find room for something else."

My Higher Self paused. "How long do you think we have been sitting here?"

"Oh, I don't know. About an hour?" I had been sitting with my back to the clock and had spent most of the conversation in an attentive daze.

"Look at the clock," insisted my Higher Self.

I craned my neck around to look at the clock. It was nearly lunchtime. I was astonished. I'd lost all track of linear time.

"You never said a truer word," replied my Higher Self. "The track that is lost is time, and it's breaking up, fading away. You are beginning to step outside time, realizing the limitation it represents."

"Well, I thought I'd be bored staying here all day," I admitted.

"We can still arrange that," joked my Higher Self.

"No, I don't want to. I choose otherwise! But I am curious to know where time goes."

"Does it matter? Time is only a figment of your linear imagination."

"That is easy for you to say because it doesn't exist from your perspective. But it's becoming more and more obvious that my experiences speed up and slow down when I least expect them to. Time used to be such a comfortable limitation. Lately I've felt like I'm going out of control with so little time or the fear of too much."

"I hadn't heard you complain before. It seemed to me you were enjoying the freedom."

"Well, I was. Or rather, I will be. Well actually, I am. It's just such a curious transition. I am adapting though." I confirmed my commitment by screwing my face up, as if that made it greater.

"There you go, getting upset with your times in one sentence. No wonder past, present and future make one tense," my Higher Self laughed. "Get the joke?"

"Yes, I get it. All times are running together and who am I to try and measure them or separate them?" I sighed, letting out the breath I didn't know I'd been holding.

"Who are you, indeed? What is your world coming to when the line you were following starts dissolving? ...I jest." My Higher Self paused. "You know deep down that the only line worth following is within your Heart; a cosmic guideline; never a limit; a devotion that will connect all times, all lifetimes and reunite you with your true nature."

"Yes, yes. If I am to become unlimited then I can't hide behind time or any other constraint. It's just that consciously choosing to take away the finishing post or even the beginning is just so odd... a loss of dependability. But in my Heart I understand that I will sense when it's the end or the beginning; I won't require linear time to tell me."

"Feeling cosmic cycles helps you adapt to Cosmic Timing," replied my Higher Self. "To research Limitation as fully as you have, linear time was the most limited structure within which to constrain your experiences. It was literally a track that you could slide up and down but never deviate from. Now that you are choosing to spend more and more of that perceived linearity within your IAM, it's not so much a question of where linear time is going, it's more a matter of realizing that you are stepping outside of it more and more often.

"There is no time within IAM. The result is that your experience of Linear Time is dissolving. If your thoughts are being energized within your IAM, you will be out of space and time. You may not have the time any more, but you certainly don't have its constraints either."

I suddenly excited at the prospects of no time. "Am I becoming a time traveler then?"

"Not in the sense of traveling back to previous centuries of experience in the physical world, or dipping into a lifetime where you were comfortable, famous or powerful," said my Higher Self soberly. "As you welcome more and more unlimited vibrations back into your energy field, you are creating a vortex that is spinning out of control and into Love. There would be no point in visiting your past, nor for that matter your perceived future, because you have chosen to shift your awareness and experience out of the limitation of linear time altogether.

"All of the structures that have maintained limited control are melting. It doesn't matter if you are grinding to a halt or flying apart, you are experiencing the acceleration required to change your Limitation into liberation. If you were to try and view this shift from your current perspective, it would be like saying you are in the middle of all linear times, able to access your past, present and future all together. But what would be the point?"

"It would be like taking a walk down Memory Lane just for the sake of it," I interjected.

"Yes," said my Higher Self encouragingly, "and as you move out of Limitation, Memory Lane becomes closed. All that remains is to consolidate the allowance required to live and create without linear time."

"And my Ego isn't happy about this. It's like I've taken away one of it's favorite possessions?"

"Exactly. The challenge is not to disperse yourself through Ego by indulging in linear time. Dwelling in the past or projecting yourself into the future draws you out of your IAM and scatters your energy. When you can learn from the moment that is your Now, you will break through the limitations of linear time."

"Simple, really," I smiled. "It can be achieved in a moment."

"Absolutely," came the reply.

"I was only joking, Higher Self. It's hard for me to believe at the moment. Something so simple appears incredibly complicated from here."

"Well, embracing the concept of 'no time' is possible, it's just that it isn't probable for you at present."

"But the idea of the Now is definitely growing on me... or perhaps I would say growing within me. I doesn't panic me that I might be losing time forever, nor that I might not be making the best use of time. So that is progress, right?" I queried.

"Yes. Part of the key to believing in the Now is to stop measuring the distance between yourself and your creations; to know from the moment you release your intentions that their result is flowing to you. All you are required to do is release yourself from the perceived time this takes and then it will happen in no time." My Higher Self fell silent.

"I believe you," I said hurriedly, "I just have no idea how to apply this. It's so easy to slip back into Ego and fight a lack of time or congratulate myself on how long I've spent on something, thinking that will make it more valuable."

"Indeed. Ego will always react to 'no time' by telling you that you're the inadequate one; you're the one that misses out by not having time to coordinate your creations and experiences. Ego will tell you it simply isn't possible to create more by having less time. But this is Ego law, not Cosmic Wisdom. You will find that without linear time, your life won't be a shadow of its former self; it won't have targets, deadlines and scarcities. It is Ego that is running out of time because you don't want the limits it offers anymore. You want flow, liberation, flexibility. Linear time isn't enough any more; it can't coordinate the Grand Flow. Only the Now can do that."

I was temporarily distracted from the conversation by the sound of a blender. I looked towards the counter and saw the waitress bring out two smoothies. Conscious that my mind had been wandering, I reconnected with the conversation. "Sorry, what were you saying?" I asked.

"The blender said it for me," beamed my Higher Self.

"What do you mean?" I was completely lost.

"When you blend Limitation with higher awareness you get a mixture of energy that can have either Ego or IAM at its center. It's a bit like porridge—you get the porridge that flows, and then you get the lumpy bits. The lumpy bits are Ego's contribution to the mixture. So you've been talking to both Ego and Heart. You are more able now to detach from the objections of your Ego, but also to learn from them at the same time. You aren't reacting to the lumpy bits any more, you're stirring them into the mix, accepting them for what they represent—the dissolving of Ego."

"So, if I understand this correctly…" I began slowly. "When Ego is in the center, it's a tense process filled with protests as Ego projects and distracts the mind or shouts out into my world, demonstrating the fear of losing linear time. Plenty of people have said to me, for example, 'You can't do that' or 'There isn't enough time' or 'What do you mean you don't remember? I only told you a minute ago.' And all of this is the dissolving of time while Ego tries to stop the process?"

"Yes. And so it continues. Your best way of returning to your IAM is to leave your Ego to rant and rave through your environment by itself. The more detached you are, the less your Ego will be able to disturb you. You know in your Heart that you aren't losing time just a limitation that has out-lived its purpose."

"But if I react or take these fear outbursts personally, let's say, then I will be attaching myself to those big lumps of fear and I'll get exhausted by what could happen rather than what is the true reality," I added.

"Yes. So look at the lumpy bits in the flow as the interesting pieces, the bits that offer the return to Life and RealLife. If you can transmute these lumpy bits into your flow by recycling them, changing your mind about the passing limits they represent, then you will always benefit from them. There's no fuel you can't use, you are just required to adapt. So during these periods of adaptation you are best served in your IAM. If you can keep your awareness there then you will experience the least amount of disturbance."

"Have you ever looked into the center of a blender?" asked my Higher Self. The question appeared to be disconnected from our main discussion, but I went with the flow.

"No, I haven't. But is it similar to a whirlpool?" I wondered.

"Yes. So if you are at the center of the whirlpool, you might well perceive that you are standing still instead of getting bumped around in the outer extremes of the vortex. This is why it is so helpful to be in your IAM during times of disruption."

"But Ego would try and tempt me out of the peace of my IAM to be where the action is. It would say that being peaceful was doing nothing and contributing nothing."

"You're learning. So tell me, what would happen if you go to the outer extremes?"

"I could get entangled with what is being recycled — fear, resistance, control — and give all this potential fuel back to my Ego in the form of a fit of depression, anger or inertia."

"Certainly. So at maximum acceleration, the smoothest journey is the one of calm and balance, even if there are periods of major disturbance. Remember, just because you don't like it doesn't mean it isn't helpful. Everything in your world of creations can help you to better understand your unlimited creative power."

"So if there are exaggerated aspects in my environment — people or sensations — or I feel tempted to be reactive or move into extremes, being in my IAM will stop me going on Ego detours."

"Exactly. You will learn to be at peace during such changes and this will allow them to happen both elegantly and efficiently."

"And again, I won't know when these lumpy bits are going to come up. I am required to trust guidance in helping me deal with them when they happen?" I added.

"Yes. Trust is another one of the keys that opens the door to IAM. You always have everything you require in such instances. However, it's tempting to think Ego is winning because it tells you that you are doing nothing to help yourself, when in truth you are 'being' in order to gain maximum acceleration."

"So I must be going pretty fast now," I said. "There's so much G-force my head hurts!"

I slumped forward onto the table, putting my chin on crossed arms. I was almost exhausted by the learning of each moment. This was truly getting the most out of time by being without it! My mind was reeling at the realization of how so much of my mental capacity was wrapped up in linear time. I was spending so many thoughts each day maintaining something that could only help me perpetuate my Limitation.

Liquid lunch

"The waitress is looking in your direction. Do you want any lunch?" asked my Higher Self, sensing I was floating between my Heart and my mind.

"Probably a good idea, but I don't know what I want." I sat up straight and listened to my body's lunch request… "I'll have a fruit juice." I motioned for the waitress to come over.

"Would you like to look at the lunch specials?" she asked.

"No thanks, I'll just have a fruit juice, please. What have you got that's freshly squeezed?"

"We have orange, apple or carrot."

"I'll have an apple juice please."

As I ordered, I cast a glance around the café and noticed that none of the breakfast traffic had been replaced with any lunchtime custom. It was one o'clock and yet I was their only customer. All the kitchen conversations were amplified as the empty space echoed my order.

"Look at all the space," I said to my Higher Self.

"Indeed. It's amazing how much space you create when you haven't got time… linear time, that is!"

I smiled to myself as the waitress arrived with my drink and the bill simultaneously. I thanked her. But instead of drinking my juice, I simply stared into it, watching the apple pulp separating from the froth. I looked at the clock and saw that barely ten minutes had elapsed since I last looked.

"Feeling bored?" asked my Higher Self.

"Not exactly… All right, if I'm honest, my mind is trying

to take me on a boredom detour. I know it's been much more rewarding going around in these ever-increasing circles of wisdom than I would ever have guessed, but things are beginning to drag a little. It feels like the learning curve just got a bit steeper and I'm not convinced I want to carry on any further. I think I've been on the spin cycle long enough," I concluded.

"That's your choice," came the guidance.

"And yet," I continued, "I feel like I'm giving up on all that we've talked about. Can you tell me in one simple phrase what is going on?"

"Struggle-free creation," announced my Higher Self.

"That may be so, but it doesn't feel like that right now," I reacted.

"Well, struggle-free doesn't mean effort-free. This experience requires some effort because you are allowing simplicity. When you stay in your IAM for more extended periods, everything becomes soaked in a simplicity that brings both your creations and your resistance to you more quickly. However, it also reduces the amount of true effort you exert in the process. The tables are now turned; you are currently feeling the effort that Ego is exerting to keep conscious change at bay.

"Now you've taken up residence in your IAM, your Ego is telling you that centeredness is boring and pointless. Your Life has lost its challenge and you've lost your pep. Ego tempts you with different aspects of itself, hoping to ensnare you. For example, ever-shortening cycles of fashion, politics, relationships and entertainment all designed to shatter the peace you have created and to absorb you back into Ego sameness.

"If you want this then all you are required to do is choose it. If you want to maintain your peace then think of these inner conflicts as Ego jumping up and down trying to attract your attention. You can see it, you can feel it and even hear it, yet you don't endorse or react to it. You are unmoved, not because you are insensitive but because you simply choose to employ yourself differently—peacefully. When Ego realizes it doesn't have an audience, it will stop."

My Higher Self paused as if checking my rate of understanding and how it was affecting my internal wiring. "Anyway enough said, I'll leave you to your drink. You know where to find me." The voice began to fade. But no sooner had I settled into silence than I called my Higher Self back.

"You rang?" came the reply.

"Yes. I don't want to leave myself dangling in thin air. You know... that place between understanding and realization." I shivered at the thought of the disconnection, even felt a sense of guilt at letting myself down. "So, can we complete what we were discussing? That is what I choose," I added, doing my best to confirm my commitment.

"Certainly," said my Higher Self, mimicking my businesslike tone, as if adjusting the furniture in my IAM Center in preparation for my visit. "Don't stand outside though. Come across the threshold of your IAM and close the door; there's a bit of a draft."

I relaxed into my IAM, surprised at my command of commitment.

My Higher Self continued. "As you make conscious progress, you start to see how so much of your world was built on 'doing' without a purpose. You were missing in action because 'doing' was so comforting. You invested your energy in habits and inabilities so that you could hold on to struggle. You were told that you wouldn't get anything unless you worked hard for it and Ego was happy to reinforce your conditioning through every action you took.

"Now the reign of unconscious doing has come to an end, you can replace it with conscious thought and an elegant use of an ever-expanding energy flow. Being efficient is no longer defined as cramming more into the same space or time. It is the ability to flow with your environment and yourself at higher and higher energy levels while simultaneously recycling Ego obstacles. Ego can never support you in this multi-directional expansion because that was never its purpose. Does that answer your question?"

"It certainly does. It supplies the missing piece in my boredom puzzle," I replied.

I felt someone standing next to me. The waitress had returned. "Do you want anything else?" she asked, standing next to me self consciously as if there was something more.

"No thanks," I replied, thinking she would leave. She stayed. "I just have to ask you to settle up," she continued awkwardly, "because my shift is ending. I hope you don't mind me asking, but... are you waiting for someone? You've been here a really long time."

"Well..." I was surprised by the question.

"Oh, your friend didn't show up?" she interjected, as if feeling sorry for me.

"No, not exactly. I wanted some time to myself, to get some direction. You know how it is."

The waitress looked as though she had no idea how it was, picking up the bill and notes and turning towards the till.

"Do you want the change?" she asked looking over her shoulder.

I smiled as I remembered a sign I once saw in a café that read 'If you don't want change, leave it here'.

"Do you want the change?" she repeated.

"Oh yes, I want change... just not that change," I smiled, caught in my private flash back.

She looked at me blankly.

"Oh sorry." I sat up in my seat. "Please keep the change," I replied, quickly focusing my attention. "Just one question: What time do you close?"

"Oh, not for ages yet. You've got plenty of time to find yourself. Good luck," she said, almost laughing secretively as if to say 'I know where you are — lost!'

"Thanks," I said, attempting to sound more normal than her appraisal of me.

It felt really awkward admitting that I was spending time with myself. I am quite sure she felt sorry for me. I tuned back in to my Higher Self.

"She may, she may not. What's important is how you are feeling and how you choose to observe your response."

"Embarrassed and cornered," I laughed at the ridiculous nature of my situation. "What could I have said?" I continued. "She would never have believed me if I'd told her my friend had arrived, that it was my Higher Self and you were in my IAM."

"That is your assumption. If you didn't speak your truth, how can you serve yourself and the waitress in understanding it?" answered my Higher Self succinctly.

"Okay, I surrender! What you're saying is that if I don't believe in myself enough to speak my truth, then how can I expect others to believe me?"

"Indeed," replied my Higher Self in a smiling voice.

"But honestly, Higher Self, sometimes it feels really, really tempting to follow the herd, forget about listening to my higher guidance and to define myself through others; to fit in, be popular, become important in mundane ways rather than appearing a freak," I added.

"But where would you be fitting in?" enquired my Higher Self.

"Into Limitation..." and I began to smile.

"Do you remember when you did fit in?" My Higher Self was enticing me into a deeper understanding.

"I'd have to open up Memory Lane to do that. I suppose I almost can."

"Do you remember when you went to parties and

weddings because you thought you had to? Do you remember when you went to a family function because you didn't want to hurt your brother's feelings?"

"Yes. That was when I loved others and myself only enough to lie to them or withhold my truth for fear of hurting them. I thought I was under scrutiny by everyone because I felt differently and didn't really want to be with them. Now I know that I was perpetuating an Ego lie, using my resources fearfully rather than lovingly. Now I want every one of my co-creations to come from Love, not from obligation or fear. No more victim consciousness for me, even if it appears to be the most attractive option. So in a way it's a good job there isn't any linear time because I would be here for a millennium sorting through my detachments!" I replied, raising my eyebrows towards the ceiling.

My Higher Self ignored my attempt at humor. "Well that was then and this is Now. We have come full circle. That's what you wanted, wasn't it?.. to end consciously; end with completion? Feel an ending rather than measuring an end using a scale or a time limit? So here it is. Do you want to leave now?" asked my Higher Self.

"I don't really mind, I am at peace here, now. What do you want to do?" I surprised myself with my detached response.

"What about going for a drive?" suggested my Higher Self.

"I thought you said we weren't going to use the car today."

"Be surprised! That's what the acceleration from moment to moment brings. More opportunities than you could ever control within your mind! So why don't we go in search of the other kind of acceleration?"

"Why not? I'm ready," I said, jumping to my feet, key in hand.

Moving out and moving on

I felt sad when I returned to the hotel. The day's roller coaster of emotion ended here. The hotel would be the only other witness to the end of my cycle of learning. I could stay another day but I knew there was no point in putting off a new beginning. The 'Now' was calling me to stay within it rather than lapse into a nostalgic time warp that reminded me of the first time I ever left home.

As I entered room eleven for the last time, the whole room was swirling as if preparing to flow down a wormhole and transform into a completely new reality. There was only enough time in space to collect my belongings before familiarity dissolved around me. This was a turning point in my journey; the first moment when I knew that my lack of destination was irrelevant.

Living in the Now didn't require a plan so much as an understanding and a conscious awareness of my co-creations. Its uncertainty was actually its flow. What I would have judged as transitory and inconsequential in the past had become a significant part of my experience without any planning or prior knowledge. My Heart, not my mind, was helping me understand what was significant in each of my moments.

The hotel room wasn't much to many, and I'd been completely resistant to it at first, but now I couldn't remember living anywhere else. A wave of peace passed through me as I acknowledged the true meaning of 'Home is where the Heart is' and that I could create it anywhere. It was simply a matter of choice.

I opened the draws and wardrobe to check I hadn't forgotten anything. I hadn't… save perhaps how I'd grown up while staying in room eleven.

"Well it's all part of the growing up process," whispered my Higher Self gently. "No single experience is more significant than any other, it's simply that you are recognizing the steps that you've taken here and now while you've been consolidating your progress in this place."

"So all the experiences are equally valuable because they all make up my understanding of Now... the 'why me, why here, why now?' of it all."

"Yes. You've been emerging from your spiritual adolescence all the way along. Now you are maturing into spiritual adulthood."

"But that doesn't mean I have to mature into being sensible and realistic?"

"No. Those are limits you used to aim for and exist by in Limitation. Maturity in this place is the ability to remain in your IAM center as your awareness expands; to recycle even bigger chunks of Ego without reverting to 'limited' type. There's no going back now."

"Good. I choose progress. Time to go," I whispered to my Higher Self.

As I entered the main reception, I walked straight into the middle of a full-blown argument. One of the hotel guests was accusing the manager of giving her room away to another guest when she'd booked it three weeks before.

"I don't want to change," she insisted. "I don't care if you are offering me a room upgrade, it's the principle here. I bothered to book in advance and I want the room I reserved." The would-be guest's face was a picture of self righteous aggression.

"As I've already explained, that room is taken," said the manager. There is no guarantee of the specific room number when you make a booking. But to compensate, we will give you a superior room at the same rate. I am truly sorry for the inconvenience." The manager was standing his ground. I wanted to intervene as the new guest was clearly over-reacting, but my Higher Self intervened before I could.

"They don't require your judgments, nor do you require their conflict. If you rush in, whether to defend or condone, all you'll be doing is scattering your energy," advised my Higher Self firmly.

"Why? I'm not a victim of what's happening around me," I protested, beginning to soak up the dramatic atmosphere.

"No, but you will allow your energy to flow into external conflict as soon as you start to judge who is right and who is wrong. All you are required to do in these moments is value peace and remain centered. When both of them realize what they are creating, they will be able to choose an alternative. Until then, allow them the experience of conflict and perhaps they will discover choice: the choice to spend their energy on creation, not depletion."

The argument continued unabated as both the voices and the debate began to heighten.

"So what about fighting for a cause?" I continued. "There are plenty of genuine causes."

"The only way you can help a cause is through peace. No genuine cause can be supported by conflict," replied my Higher Self eloquently.

So I stood patiently until both realized they had an audience. All fell silent at once; my Higher Self as well as the verbal sparring partners.

"Could I pay my bill please?" I asked softly.

"One moment," said the manager to the guest. "Would you mind if I serve this customer first?" He gestured towards me.

"Fine, go ahead," said the guest, running out of verbal ammunition.

"Which room was it?" asked the manager, glad of the let up in hostilities. I handed him the key. "Oh yes," he said, regaining his cool. "Number eleven. How would you like to pay?"

"Cash," I replied.

The atmosphere in reception began to lighten and the polarized intensity eased. The guest had lost her appetite for conflict and the manager saw a truce in sight. As I left, I heard him saying, "Would you prefer number seventeen? It's next door to the room you booked and is very convenient to the pool."

"No," said the customer. "I'll take the superior one you suggested."

As soon as I sat in the car everything felt different. There appeared to be more space around me and within the interior. What a weird sensation, I observed. It was as if the space around me had become fluid. I waited until I adjusted to my spatial rift and then started the car.

"I'm not alarmed," I said, "just curious. Why does the car interior feel and look so different?"

"Well, let's put it this way: you are going with the flow, and now you are beginning to see it."

"Thank you, Higher Self. Your words seem to make total sense but I have no idea what you've just explained."

"I quite understand. This is, after all, Cosmic Sense, not your limited common sense!"

"Well, Cosmic or otherwise, I trust the car still functions the same. Where are we going?" I asked, excited to be on the road again.

For the first time on our journey my Higher Self was bombarding me with specifics. Quite a change to the meandering philosophy of earlier stages of our journey.

"Go along this road for about eleven more kilometers then turn right before the lay-by on the left. Follow the road around to the right and you'll see a house in the trees a little ahead of you. We're going there."

This was the shortest excursion yet. I found the house set back into the trees naturally flowing with the contour of the hills. It shone white through the green.

"Are we going to stay here tonight?" I enquired.

"It's an option, but we don't have to stop here. Go and see how you feel inside, first," came the guidance.

The front door was open and when I entered there was a welcoming hint of roses and lavender. I immediately felt reassured and welcomed. The appearance of the house was deceptive as it was much larger than its façade portrayed. The entrance opened out immediately into a very large seated area with a kitchen off to the left and an entertainment area on the right. The back wall of the dining area was one continual glass panel with sliding doors leading out into the wilderness behind.

"There's so much space." I was astonished.

"Yes, its designer was very interested in freedom of expression. You have all the space you require here to be yourself. How do you feel?" asked my Higher Self with increased curiosity.

"Well, it's certainly different. It feels so clear. There's no clutter; there isn't anything that doesn't have a purpose. Yet the space is beautifully crafted as though it's designed to stimulate your awareness and intuition."

"Glad it appeals to you. I take it you'll be staying then?"

I said yes immediately.

"Don't bother bringing your things in from the car as everything you require is here."

Surprised, but happy to believe my Higher Self, I walked over to the sofa and fell into its embracing softness. I couldn't remember when I had last felt this relaxed.

——— ——— ———

When I awoke the house was in darkness. This sudden absence of light caught me off guard. I quickly walked in the direction of the door to find the light switches. "Do you need some light?" whispered my Higher Self.

"Yes, I do," I replied, thinking my Higher Self would supply my request. The room remained dark.

"Where are the light switches?" I questioned, becoming agitated.

"Just let your eyes acclimatize; there's nothing to fear. The more you need something, the less likely you are to create it," came the guidance.

"I can't think about that now," I protested, "I need to find the light switches!" I was becoming edgy. "I can't see a thing."

"You're getting warmer..." said my Higher Self, as if we were playing Blind-man's-Bluff. "Warmer still..."

I was approaching the window.

"Okay. This isn't some cruel game." There was now more than a hint of sarcasm in my voice.

"On the contrary. Blind-man's-Bluff is the perfect analogy," countered my Higher Self.

"So where's the light hiding?" I challenged.

"But why should that bother you? What are you afraid of? Frightened you'll be overcome by the darkness," replied my Higher Self, bypassing my question.

I stopped where I stood.

"The light is always there. You're the only one keeping yourself in the dark. When you are in need, you forget all the other alternatives around you," My Higher Self switched from humor to compassion. It broke my silence.

"So what other alternatives do I have? Are there any candles near?" I began to focus on my challenge instead of my fear.

"Yes. One big circular one." I could feel my Higher Self smiling.

"Well, nothing is coming to mind," I replied, dejectedly.

"Why don't you try your Heart," added the voice.

"Still nothing." I fell silent, expanding my search.

"Up a bit... higher... higher... lift your sights," encouraged my Higher Self. "What do you see?"

"The moon," came my answer.

I reached out in front of me and felt some curtains. Pulling them back, I was greeted by a full moon shining almost as bright as day. I sat in its rays, transfixed by its wholeness. 'Simplicity outshines everything,' I thought. 'The answers are always so simple.'

"So... need made me temporarily blind? Is that it?" I answered.

"Yes," responded my Higher Self. "You became incapable because your rational mind was a blank. Your Ego was trying to escalate your need, get you to focus on your fear, not on alternatives. You aren't used to relying on your creativity, the true genius within you."

"Can you elaborate?" I continued.

"When you need something, you believe you will be incomplete without it. Need is the Ego's version of want and is often mistaken for want. It originates in your mind and drives you to create from fear. When you want something, you are not driven by Ego, you are allowing of Heart and you focus your energy into what you believe and trust is possible in that moment."

"So want keeps your creative ability expanding and need causes it to narrow, to constrict?"

"Yes. Look down the corridors of your mind into the past. How many actions did you take in physicality because you believed you needed to?"

"All of them... until I woke up and realized I had a choice," I answered.

"Did you help your mother because she needed you to or because you wanted to help her? Did you study at college because you believed you needed the qualification or because you wanted to learn about your chosen subject? Did you surround yourself with household possessions because you thought you needed them to comfort you or because you wanted to use them or fill your world with beauty?"

"That's a lot of questions but I get the point. Yes I built much of my world on the fear of not surviving it rather than on the joy of experiencing it," I confirmed. "Until now, the choice wasn't so clear. It was lost in the gloom of Ego and conditioning. What I know now is that I have a choice and the intention behind my creative choice is the switch that illuminates the abundance, ease and joy in all creations. There is always illumination, it's just that sometimes I can be tricked by Ego into burying myself in the gloom of victimhood."

There was a pause in the conversation,

"So ask yourself what you want, not what you fear being without," clarified my Higher Self.

"I want to switch the lights on," I replied firmly.

Illumination

The room was suddenly ablaze with what appeared to be every light fitting possible. I squinted my eyes in reaction to the intensity.

"What an adjustment," I muttered. "Darkness and then complete illumination. Is there a dimmer switch?" I squeaked.

"Blinded by your own brilliance?" observed my Higher Self.

"How is that possible?" I queried as I began to adjust.

"Well, you're the one who's created this degree of illumination. If you hadn't, this demonstration wouldn't have been possible," added my Higher Self.

"But how was it such a surprise?" I was curious.

"One of those Initiations creeping up on you again."

"But this Initiation had a different flavor; it wasn't like the others. Was it an overall change instead of just a change within a specific energy band?" I was surprised by my precision.

"Bingo! You've just passed your perception and observation exams!"

"So where to next? Where does this greater Initiation take us?"

"It takes us to enjoyment. We aren't going to rush out into the future just now though. Let's celebrate your progress. Are you hungry?" enquired my Higher Self.

"Now you ask, I am really, really hungry. Did you read my mind?" I replied, not really thinking what I'd said.

"Well, I am privy to a little insider information, now and again. Call it overflow," chuckled the voice.

"Are you going to help me instantaneously create a beautiful three course meal for one?" I said hopefully.

"Well, open the fridge and all the ingredients you want will be there. All you are required to do is cook it."

"So, still some manual labor involved? I'm obviously not a fully qualified Magician yet."

"Well, more like sous-chef. Every Master Magician undergoes an apprenticeship. Are you trying to make me redundant?" joked my Higher Self.

"Now, would I do that?" I teased. "Well, not quite yet, anyway!" I added.

The house had everything that I could want within it. Be it cooking utensils, music or beautiful decor, everything that appeared was what I would have chosen. It was almost unnerving.

"You know me inside out," I said while relaxing after dinner. "Did you create this house especially for me?"

"Call it a coordinated joint effort, mostly created by you," replied my Higher Self. "I helped with the bits that were temporarily lost in translation. Take all this as a compliment. The house represents how well you know yourself and what you want. So, from your assessments, it would appear that you know yourself fairly well."

"But how could I have done that when I didn't know about this house?"

"Just because you didn't know about it doesn't negate the fact that it is possible. Remember that you've spent most of this journey thinking outside the cube, and what have you found there? Much more than you ever thought possible! There are plenty of gloriously fulfilling vibrations available to you. Some of them you may not have encountered yet, but that doesn't negate their presence in the Universe."

"But how could it come together so well? Surely my mind must have had some input?" I persisted.

"Yes—a concerted effort to deconstruct itself! Less mind, more flow! The more open-minded you have become along this journey, the less structures you have used within your mind. You've literally cleared more space to think differently. Don't assume mind is self discipline. Mind is merely structure and the will within it can be used by Ego or Heart."

"What do you mean?" My mind was resisting the wisdom.

"Self discipline, not your mind, has supported you in coordinating your efforts. Mind used to help your Ego coordinate its efforts in maintaining control of your experiences, regulating your limits and fears. But with less limits and more open-mindedness you've become more accustomed to self discipline."

"I understand. It's my old mental conditioning that tells me I can't do anything without the mind. I can do a lot with an open uncluttered mind but that potential can only be unlocked by self discipline—that's the key to focusing my efforts. So to rephrase this, you helped me develop the tools and abilities that were just under the surface of myself. I might not have been aware of them and they weren't in my mind, but they were still there if I wanted to use them. So this is a kind of final practical; a finale after all the exploration?"

"Yes. It is a culmination of everything that you want at this time; a reflection of your own creation capabilities, your requirements and your ability to integrate them."

"But these will change and the house will change?" I questioned.

"Yes. When you change, all your creations will change to reflect your progress."

"So this has been created mostly by me, for me."

"Yes," confirmed my Higher Self.

"But isn't that selfish?" I questioned.

"Why?" replied my Higher Self.

"Well, I've concentrated all my thoughts on something for me," I continued.

"Why is that selfish?" asked my Higher Self, stressing the question's meaning.

"Because surely I should be thinking of others before myself," I replied tentatively, already uneasy with my answer.

"What about thinking of others and yourself simultaneously?" came the suggestion.

"How can I do that?" I was perplexed at such an alien solution.

"It's simple. All you are required to be is balanced, then your thoughts will be balanced. One of the greatest misunderstandings that has been created by Ego to fortify Limitation is that giving in to your heartfelt wants is selfish. Religions and social conventions have emphasized that those who have achieved the complete release of Limitation have done so through martyrdom. This definition of service is created by Ego, for Ego.

Service isn't martyrdom, it is an activity that is chosen, just like any other. It can be a great pleasure if undertaken through choice and allowance. If you spent all of your life giving to others without giving to yourself, then sooner or later you would become exhausted trying to create what you thought others wanted and depriving yourself of the flow of energy required to become unlimited. Remember your Mini? The number 8? And what goes around comes around? Giving and receiving are the actions which create this number."

"Yes, but I'm really slow. I still don't understand why."

"Because you would be out of balance and out of the Cosmic Flow if you gave without ever receiving. You would be starving your energy field by trying to give yourself away rather than acknowledging when you want to give to you. You wouldn't be valuing you and you would be resisting your part of the Cosmic Flow."

"So If I won't receive in balance with giving then I would literally be resisting the flow of the Universe; I wouldn't be letting what goes around, come back around?"

"Precisely."

"So really, what those of old were saying was not give until you drop but give joyously without conditions; give because you want to, not because you have to."

"Exactly. But many still researched what it was like to spend lifetimes doing only for others and never experiencing giving to themselves. Many have carried the burden of this imbalance from lifetime to lifetime simply because they believed there was no other alternative. Ego substantiated this through sensations such as guilt, fear of rejection, desire for approval and the need to be needed.

"When you progress through the fear of appearing weak, selfish or unwanted, then a miracle occurs. A change of mind and Heart turns being selfish into being self loving. No longer are you worried about trying to make another happy nor about feeling embarrassed because you're doing something for yourself. You are allowing creation to flow, embracing the ability to serve yourself and others as the opportunities arise instead of maintaining an Ego default that imbalances all experiences."

"So that's why I can't make another person happy," I said, feeling a wave of realization. "Service is a choice, just like anything else. If we start serving others how we think they would want to be served, instead of asking them, then in truth we won't be able to help, we will just be controlling through our own expectations and assumptions."

"Exactly. Ego is very good at convincing you that helping another equals giving someone what you would want rather than helping them create what they want. This is just another Ego misunderstanding. No one can change another person's life, they can only support change; be the inspiration. The ultimate choice to change rests with each individual.

"Part of your research trip was to gather experiences on an individual level. If anyone were to try and serve you by creating on your behalf, they would be robbing you of your unique creation perspective. To remain in balance and serve unconditionally, you are required to be honest with yourself whilst allowing others their chosen level of fulfillment."

"So what about those who never give, only take?" I changed direction.

"They will come to a point in their experience where they may perceive that they are forced to give; or that they are losing everything because there is no incoming energy, no one giving to them. But as always this is the result of an Ego misunderstanding. It is simply that they are at the other end of their imbalance. Their lack of giving is returning to them. What has gone around has come back around. They are now required to face their fear of giving to bring the flow back into balance."

"So the most important element behind all giving and receiving is the intention?" I sought a recap.

"Yes. To correct imbalance, first the intention behind the flow needs to be known."

"So being self loving is recognizing when to give and when to receive, not hijacking someone else's creation stream or depleting your own by serving others indiscriminately or continuously."

"Indeed. True service isn't martyrdom, it's a joy because it's a harmonious state of being. When you serve unconditionally, you do it because your Heart's in it, not because you are forcing yourself or being forced. Whenever you give, think of yourself as guiding the universal flow rather than taking energy away from your own personal creation capability. And think of helping yourself as being as important as helping another. If doing anything for you brings out feelings of discomfort, weakness or anger then you have found the threshold of resistance that Ego has developed in order to insulate you from your own power.

"Balancing your creation flow will never take energy away from another because the flow is unlimited and unending. A state of dynamic balance will always give you the opportunity to expand in harmony.

The way home

"So can I ask you again, where are we going now?" I returned to my previous question.

"Do you expect an answer?" replied my Higher Self mysteriously.

"No, I want an understanding because I'm sure there isn't a destination."

"A subtle and wise distinction. Your journey is flowing into the subtle aspects of Self," replied my Higher Self.

"So which tools will I be using in this cycle?"

"All… plus more that you don't currently believe you have but you will find in the flow."

"Is our relationship going to change as a result of these discoveries?" I began to feel deep sadness that brought tears to my eyes. "Does this mean you're going to leave?" I became distressed as tears turned to sobs. "We had such a great arrangement. Why change it now?"

"Because our relationship has changed and to accommodate the progress that you have made, change is essential. The sense of loss you are feeling now is only the fear of recycling what was becoming a dependable and personable friendship. But this is not the true nature of our relationship. It is a stop along the way home to RealLife. Freezing our relationship in a particular form just because you like it or are frightened to change it only serves Ego. Think of how you have changed during your journey—is this change not the perfect reflection of that?"

"Yes it is. But what will we become in the next phase of our relationship?" I asked, the tears beginning to subside.

"Our mature nature. Instead of growing old together, we will grow wise together. You are no longer a spiritual infant, you've grown up—not in a somber or cynical way but in the sense of spiritual maturity. This gives you a wider choice and the tools to command your increased creative power.

"Maturity in RealLife means you are recognizing the reflection of your ability in your world and working with it. To achieve this you are required to be more detached. Instead of taking your hand and showing you the way, we are now walking into a guided companionship; a maturing fellowship as your awareness, of yourself and RealLife becomes more tangible. You know that all your choices are your own, it's just that from this point on; you will be assuming full responsibility for them and your creations. You will still have your guidance but you will require it less and less. The job of guiding yourself to fulfillment and unlimited creativity will eventually return to you."

My Higher Self paused as if considering a question while simultaneously assessing the degree of disturbance it would make in my mind.

"You want to become a Master of the Alchemy Of Change; become an instantaneous creator, right?" It was as if my Higher Self was carefully crafting the questions.

"Yes, I do. I want to create instantaneously, joyously and abundantly."

"Do you believe you can do it?" asked my Higher Self seriously.

"Yes. With your help, I believe I can come to that point. However, I am becoming more and more aware of the wisdom and tools that it's going to require to achieve," I replied.

"Great. An open Heart and an open mind. With these, whatever you see at this juncture as being impossible will become do-able and be-able," said my Higher Self, ignoring my hint of fatigue.

"Here's another question for you: What do you think it would be like to be able to create instantaneously right now?"

"Magical… and probably overwhelming!" I replied.

"Why do you say that?" asked my Higher Self, appearing curious.

"Because the more I've learnt on this journey, the more I realize there is to learn. I feel that if I had that power right now, I wouldn't be able to handle it; my Ego would hijack my mind and I'd be drowning in the fear of my own success or be crushed by the responsibility of such power. That kind of ability is so far reaching… Firstly the thought discipline to stabilize it is mind boggling; the clarity, surrender and honesty I'd require to actually know what I wanted… Then there's the realization that so many other aspects of my world would be made redundant in that moment. For example, if I could create anything then I wouldn't require money. Back in the physical world that part of me still inhabits, money is still a high priority. But it would become irrelevant; there would be no need to amass anything or fear loosing anything, and no point in competing for anything. This would perhaps come as a great relief because I'd probably be spending most of my unlimited flow of energy adapting to it.

"If I were going to prepare for such a state of being right now, I would start by focusing on dissolving the fear in my mind and in my thought processes. Look at me — I was frightened and distressed at the prospect of our relationship changing, simply because I was beginning to feel secure. I immediately started to think of the worst that could happen instead of the valuable progress this change in circumstances reflected!"

"Congratulations! You really are getting to know yourself better," said My Higher Self. "Just remember, the laughter, conflicts and clarifications are all part of richness of this journey, irrespective of how it might appear."

"Yes," I admitted. "Even if I didn't know I was being funny, arguing or muddled, it all came together at the right time. But of one thing I'm certain: if you'd told me all about this before I got to the Bar of Conditioning, I don't know whether I would have taken up this research project."

"It's just as well your mind and Ego had no idea how powerful your Heart is!" chuckled my Higher Self. "But that's all part of your re-wiring,"

"What do you mean by *re-wiring*?" I probed.

"It's all part of your gradual shift into spiritual adulthood. If I can just go back to the beginning of our journey..."

"Yes go on," I said almost impatiently.

"Rewiring refers to your energetics. You know that to research Existence, your physical body is still in Physicality?"

"Yep."

"So, the lowest vibration of energy is represented by physical form — Physicality. Therefore the densest part of you is your physical body. If you are going to finish your research and return to RealLife then you are going to need to recycle this part of yourself as well as the emotional and mental limits that have been part of your research."

"So this is another example of why nothing can be created nor destroyed?"

"Yes. Everything gets recycled. But you have a choice how you do this. You can carry on your research across physical lifetimes or you can make a concentrated effort now to gather all of the aspects of yourself into RealLife."

"So if I'm going to achieve that, the dense aspects such as my physical body will need to relinquish their limited nature. But being this dense, its going to take a lot of gradual shifts to be able to rearrange the physical form without destroying it?"

"Indeed. So if you are going to rewire yourself into RealLife, you are required to receive this increase in energy gently; not too much current, as it were, or you'll blow your physical fuses."

"So don't tell me—that comes from being in the Now!"

"Yes, and all the application of all the other tools and wisdoms that you've learnt on your path forward. The more aware you become, the more current you can take until you are able to induce more and more change."

"If I can put it another way," I interrupted. "I'm doing the reverse of my research in Limitation. I'm uploading all my research to the 'big mainframe in the sky'—'All That Is'—and downloading increasingly expanded versions of my software until I will be able to be in RealLife completely."

"Yes. All your Transformations and Initiations have contributed to you reconfiguring yourself to greater and greater degrees. The more unlimited software you download, the more you will experience the unlimited world."

"So if I plot my energetic progress to now... I was Existing, then I woke up to choice. This progressed into embracing conscious choice by working with you instead of just with my mind and Ego. Then I chose to apply the wisdoms that you taught me and started growing up spiritually. Listening less and less to the fears of my Ego has created more and more alternatives and rebuilt more and more of my unlimited nature."

"Carry on," said my Higher Self.

"I've had a thought revolution, moving the center of my world from Ego-focused to Heart-centered. I've rebuilt my unlimited nature to the point where I can recognize and maintain my I AM Center. I've learnt to be in the Now and to believe that I can live without struggle, fear and control."

I took a breath. "To achieve this I've discovered choice, trust, flow, self discipline, responsibility and self honesty, to name but a few tools. I've also been through the fears and resistances I harbored to be able to recycle them. Finishing my journey to the home I have now chosen — RealLife — requires more of the same: Keep on recycling; trade in the noise of Limitation for the expansion of silence, security for spontaneity and certainty for the unknown. Now I find myself arriving in the subtler aspects of self. Does that cover it all?" I concluded.

"Bravo," said my Higher Self as a round of applause echoed around the room and the light intensified. "Welcome to your own New Light."

I took a bow, adjusting to the powerful white light more readily than before.

"Would you like a drink? Something to remember your journey back to Life? One for the road, before you sleep?"

"Why not? Some water, please. I'm feeling quite thirsty after our discussion."

An amethyst goblet appeared on the dinner table. The candles flickered signaling its arrival.

"Fantastic," I clapped appreciatively.

The purple glow of the amethyst and the light of the candles mixed together until a soothing lilac mist seemed to pervade the air. I felt a sudden heaviness. I closed my eyes and relaxed into the soothing conversation with my Higher Self, almost as if the words were the walls of the house. My Higher Self's voice echoed around the room and disappeared out into the full moonshine. I heard a wave of voices rush back through the house... and then silence.

I opened my eyes and leaned forward. There was a scroll of parchment on the coffee table in front of me.

"What's this? An invitation to the Fool and Magician

party? Or perhaps it's a map of how to get to the subtle aspects of self?"

"Unroll it and see for yourself," replied a chorus of many. "Open the scroll," they urged.

I did what I was bid and found the scroll completely blank.

"Invisible ink, eh? Well it certainly adds to the mystery. Is it a riddle? Are you inviting me to more space?" I said with mock seriousness.

"It's an invitation and a contract," came the group reply.

"What kind of invitation/contract?" I said, half laughing, half serious.

"Well, you see, we all feel that you've got a lot of potential as a Researcher so we wanted to engage your services in researching the more subtle parts of Self." There was a big cheer and a raucous rendition of For Who's All Jolly Good Fellows.

"You're asking me to put my name to a complete blank? Something I have no idea about. To trust and commit to it completely?"

"Yes, that's right."

"Ok, count me in. All for one and one for all. I take it I will be writing more of my job description?"

"Yes, that is definitely going to be part of your role," agreed the invisible crowd.

"And you will be helping me with my research? My Higher Self is with you but there's a greater choice of guidance now, not just one source of help. Is that correct?"

"Yes."

"So, the subtler sides of Self. Does this mean that you can help me see your vision and you can see how to help me with developing mine?"

"Yes."

"Sounds fine. So where do we start?" I was suddenly feeling refreshed. But I already knew the answer to that question — it was here and it was now.

All for one and one for all

There was a knock at the door. Who could it be? Surrounded by shards of daylight, I didn't want to move. Caffeine was my first desire, followed closely by the hope that whoever was outside would go away. I heard an envelope slide under the door and then my peace was completely shattered by the eleven o'clock alarm of clattering shop grilles rising to meet another Thursday trading.

Forcing my aching head and protesting neck from my desk, I felt like the victim of a creative hit-and-run. I peeled off a couple of scribbled pages that must have stuck to my face during the night.

I shuffled over to the kitchen and filled the kettle. Glancing at the calendar on the kitchen cupboard I saw the twenty-ninth was ringed in red pen—the only date in the month. That was tomorrow, the day when Erica was going to call to check on my final draft.

My mini-locomotive signaled my distress as it squealed and spluttered its way to the boil. 'All powered up and nowhere to go... sounds familiar,' I thought, looking at the living room soaked in a layer of scribbled notes. 'Well those pages certainly cover a long journey.' I thought.

"Well, one thing's certain, this Thursday's child has far to go!" I muttered, "I just don't know where!" I announced, as I cleared a space to put the pot of tea on the living room table and then sank into the sofa.

The dream that had been India, a meditation in a foreign land, was fast approaching its conclusion; a conclusion currently without an end. I glanced at my desk and the floor around it. I'd been in India nearly three months and I had an inundation of scribbled observations to show for it. Was that going to be a book? I wasn't even entirely sure if I could read them myself, much less mop them up into a story. Creative oxygen was at a premium as the fear of my situation started to exhaust my alternatives. I had forty-eight hours to conjure up a finished product.

A thought raced into the very center of my panic. 'Ask for help.' I gulped down the quickly cooling tea and stood in the center of the room.

"India, Universe, everyone... help me create a book in forty-eight hours, please," I said aloud. It was now or never.

With a pounding head I began collecting up hundreds of pages and started to sort them into chapters. I didn't stop, focused and fully energized like a literary whirling dervish, hour after hour. The hands of the clock swept around until Friday came. It began much as Thursday, waking up with a stiff neck and to the sound of shop owners and the mildly hysterical commentary in my head. Sentences merged into paragraphs and paragraphs into chapter outlines. The market clock sounded two and my overall outline was complete. My self-belief reflated as I realized I had the makings of a book. By three o'clock in the afternoon 'Indian Stretchy Time', I had all the main characters. By five I had thirty semi-legible chapters. At seven the phone startled me as it rang.

I made myself comfortable on the sofa, surrendering to the outcome of the following minutes. How was I going to tell Erica? More to the point, what was I going to tell her? The telephone was becoming impatient. I was just about to answer it when a voice in my head said 'She might welcome the change you know, like you did.' I registered the comment and reached for the phone.

"Hello, Erica," I started with breezy confidence.

"Hi, how are you? Long time no speak!" she replied brusquely.

"Well I've been incredibly busy," I started.

"I don't like the sound of that kind of busy, I know you too well. What are you cooking up?"

Erica was becoming more tense and suspicious with each passing second. I took a deep breath and answered.

"A novel. I've been cooking up a novel. It's a bit of nouvelle cuisine, unlike anything I've ever written but I really believe that it's a great new direction," I rushed out my announcement, trying to fend off the inevitable opposition.

"Slow down, slow down. You're blurting! If I understand this correctly... you've written a novel instead of a travel guide?"

I waited for a tirade that would culminate in Erica trying to get down the phone and strangle me, but there was silence. I tapped the phone gently to check it was still working.

"Erica are you there?"

"God you are amazing!" she replied, almost exploding with excitement.

"I thought you'd be killing me, yourself or both of us by now!" I said, almost breaking into laughter. "Thanks for taking this complete U-turn in my writing career so well."

There was more silence. "Erica you are still there?"

"Yes I am, just a little overwhelmed. God you pick your moments, don't you? But never as well as this one. I want you to be the first to know—there's been a complete reshuffle here at the publishers. They aren't going to do the same old stuff, it's not selling as well as it was. No offence intended, but travel in general is saturated and the bottom's fallen out of historic and nostalgia journeys so they need to do something different. There's going to be a big board meeting next Thursday to discuss the future of the company. There could be redundancies and if I don't produce a creative change in direction then I could be out of a job too. You might have conjured up just the kind of magic I need to stay in the job. Congratulations to whatever crazy guru told you to go in this direction—he's a genius."

"I conjured it up myself actually!" I said with a hint of injured originality.

"Really? Well you're capable of it and, if I'm honest, your other writing was getting a bit jaded. So congratulations to you! As long as it's good… You simply can't let me down. You know that, right? This kind of material is the answer to all our prayers. It could easily get the company out of the doldrums. This is so exciting!"

"Great. Glad you can see the potential. Let me give you a little taste. It starts in India but there aren't any gurus per se in the book."

Erica interrupted me. "But shouldn't it have a guru in it? That's what India's all about, isn't it?"

"Well…" I paused, "yes and no, Erica. If you ever get out of London Land to discover India for yourself, you'll find that it supports you in becoming your own guru. That's the whole point of spirituality — finding your own truth, not someone else's. The word guru actually means *teacher* in Hindi."

But Erica seemed unimpressed with my spiritual subtleties, being intent on planning her next move. "Anyway, enough of the detail," she said impatiently, "this is costing a fortune. Get an overview and a few sample chapters finished and be in the office on Wednesday. I'll call it a brave new spiritual beginning for the travel division. I have a feeling that it is going to go down rather well! "Now don't disappoint me; this is more perfect than you know. You relaunch your career; I get a new stable of authors and a new product direction. It's perfect. Anyway, no pressure, just get those sample chapters finished."

The line went dead. I sat in shock; and then burst out laughing and started dancing around the room.

"I did it, I did it. She liked it, she liked it!!!" I laughed at the top of my lungs.

"I told you she would," came a reply. I stopped where I stood, looking around for the voice. There was silence.

"What did you say?" I questioned the voice.

"I mentioned she might mirror the change in you; she might *welcome* the change," came the reply.

I sat down on the sofa bolt upright, my heart beating so fast I thought it was going to burst. A rush of energy poured through every part of my body.

"So, it's all flooding back now? But it's quite a different experience, isn't it, when your awareness is in the physical world? The wisdom connection is much more complicated when you are navigating through the corridors of your mind. But it appears you're getting the hang of it, if that pile of papers is anything to go by. There's a lot to go on there; you've come such a long way."

Still I couldn't formulate a reply. But this didn't seem to bother the voice.

"You could, of course, write all this in one sentence," continued the voice, "but that would never do. Physicality always demands more bulk if you're going to get your point across. More means less here but, hey, that's what gets the job done. It's all a matter of density. Realization travels more slowly when it meets more resistance. Still, it'll all work out in the end. It's all about adaptation, wouldn't you say?"

I still couldn't say anything. I couldn't even coordinate my jaw, vocal chords and mind. The voice continued unperturbed, as if carrying on a conversation that embraced my silent answers.

"Well it's a great day when you manage to surprise yourself; that's really quite an achievement. Surprising yourself with the power of purposeful writing... that's an even greater achievement. Even Erica could appreciate that but, hey, I told you that already. Wonderful subject matter, this purposeful writing; a different kind of information; one that's a lot more helpful, I might add." The voice began to fade.

"Is that you, Higher Self?" I finally managed to reply as tears of joy and surprise filled my eyes.

"Yes, it's Higher Self at your service... to help you with your service."

"I thought you were supposed to be above 'I told you so'!"

"Beyond it, to be more precise. However, it managed to get your attention didn't it?"

"Absolutely. But I'm so surprised to connect with you here. I thought you couldn't come here?" I said curiously.

"Why?"

"Well, this is too dense a realm for you to be in, isn't it? There isn't enough flow, enough flexibility. Perhaps what I'm trying to say is that this is the nightmare, not the dream; there isn't enough Universal Truth here to sustain you."

"Why?" asked my Higher Self in a serious tone.

"Because..." I paused as my immature logic dissolved and was replaced by realization. "Oh, I get it. You aren't really in this density, you're in my expanded awareness. That doesn't mean you are actually here physically. So you're here and now, just not physically... here and now."

"Yes, I am Now. And I am one of the alternatives you have created for yourself while expanding your awareness. You are now able to see the gaps in this density, the truths that lie behind and beyond the fear. All the complication and difficulty is unraveling. You simply aren't as dense as you were!"

"No I'm not. I'll take that as a compliment!" I replied decisively.

"So now you are putting the old world in context with your new worlds. You are no longer reinforcing the cracks in your old world with rigidity and fear, you are choosing creativity and expansion."

"You never said a truer word. I just went through three months of fear to get here! And Now is where I am staying. So thanks for joining me."

"Thank you for accommodating me," said my Higher Self warmly. "This is quite an adventure."

"How long did it take you to get here?" I asked, immediately realizing the ridiculous nature of my question.

"Feels like an eternity," said my Higher Self whimsically, "but who's counting? I'm here now."

"So... fancy helping me with my novel?" I asked hopefully. "Could be interesting."

"It always is," said my Higher Self. "It always is. But first, sleep."

"But I've got so much to do," I said with mild panic, "I can't sleep now."

"More accurately, you've got so much to become," replied my Higher Self.

"Okay. I bow to your superior wisdom. But can this sleep be a genuine rest?" I questioned.

"Of course! When have I ever led you into fake sleep?" protested my Higher Self comically.

"More times than I can remember!" I replied cheekily.

"Well, this time will be different, you'll see. You've created a lot more options for yourself now."

As I curled up on the sofa I heard my Higher Self continue, "Besides, how are you going to finish your book if you don't sleep?"

"It sounds very appealing," I mumbled. "You could help me conjure up a finished work... help me discover my new creative direction and, who knows, maybe this will be the service?"

"Or perhaps," said my Higher Self gently, "the service is to awaken fellow Magicians from the slumbering masses."

But I was already gone, out researching the next page of my adventure.

More About the Author...

Alexandria presents workshops, seminars and private consultations around the world, inspiring and teaching the principles of the Alchemy of Change in people's day to day lives. These events include:

Discovering the Inner Wizard

A workshop which inspires you to take command of your creativity and experience the benefits of a heart-centered life.

For information, email: InnerWizard@lifeoflight.com

Harnessing the Alchemy of Change

This workshop embraces the powerful process of change that liberates blocked and stagnant energy, recycling it into fulfilling and life-changing progress.

For information, email: AlchemyOfChange@lifeoflight.com

Connecting to Natural Forces

A full day intensive this workshop initiates you into a deeper relationship with Mother Earth and explains our planet's role in the spiritual development of you and Humanity as a whole.

For information, email: Mastery@lifeoflight.com

~

   If you'd like more information about Alexandria's work, please visit: www.lifeoflight.com
   If you'd like more information about this and other books by Alexandria, please visit: www.lifeoflightmedia.com

Printed in the United Kingdom by
Lightning Source UK Ltd., Milton Keynes
140477UK00001BA/1/P

9 780908 807123